CONTEMPORARY SOCIO-LEGAL PROBLEMS

CONTEMPORARY SOCIO-LEGAL PROBLEMS

Dr. Nalini Kanta Dutta

ANMOL PUBLICATIONS PVT. LTD.
NEW DELHI-110 002 (INDIA)

ANMOL PUBLICATIONS PVT. LTD.
Regd. Office: 4360/4, Ansari Road, Daryaganj,
New Delhi-110002 (India)
Tel.: 23278000, 23261597, 23286875, 23255577
Fax: 91-11-23280289
Email: anmolpub@gmail.com
Visit us at: www.anmolpublications.com

Branch Office: No. 1015, Ist Main Road, BSK IIIrd Stage
IIIrd Phase, IIIrd Block, Bangalore-560 085 (India)
Tel.: 080-41723429 • Fax: 080-26723604
Email: anmolpublicationsbangalore@gmail.com

Contemporary Socio-Legal Problems

ISBN 978-81-261-3296-6

PRINTED IN INDIA

Printed at Atul Printers, Delhi.

Contents

Preface

The current socio-legal problems consist of different articles on the subjects of mass concern. The topics are different and so far as possible the topics connected to social and legal problems have been put together. The book deals mainly with the prevailing environment of social as well as legal problems connected to the nations with special reference to India from the perspective of social, moral and legal responsibilities of the community.

The work emphasises the importance of political and administrative responsibilities and obligations towards control and management of problems to maintain and improve the social and economic values of the community through legal implications. Crimes involving dishonesty are committed with the ultimate object of retaining ill-gotten gains. If the offenders made to know that he will not be allowed to retain his ill-acquired gains, the springs of criminality would in most cases be dried up and the prospective offender would rather give up the idea of wrongful or dishonest acquisition. This concept is applicable not only to the offences of dishonest acquisition, but also to other offences. A rapid survey of human history from pre-historic nomadic existence to the modern highly sophisticated age of science and technology established the fact that economic development is the forerunner of social changes. Various socio-legal problems are in fact reflections of the movement of times and thoughts colouring the legal horizons of the society in which we live. Since the state has become important in every field and act as big brother, I have also to examine the question of state lawlessness. In this context I have incorporated the diversified problems in view of its connection with the aspects of social and criminal environment and international conflicts giving importance of their dimensions.

The book has included such articles which are purely of an academic value such as 'Secularism in India and Uniform Civil Code,' 'Crisis of Morality in Ethical Behaviour, 'Human Rights and Humanitarian laws, 'Preventive Detention Laws, 'Narcotic Drugs: Their use and Abuse','Corruption', Terrorism', 'Nuclear Policy', 'Space Technology' etc. How can socio-legal problems be controlled or manage effectively is a common question and urge by the widespread public for an answer to this difficult question reflects not only the seriousness of the problem, but also a general reluctance to treat the matter as seriously as it deserves. The problems like white collar crime in which the rich and influential persons are involved polluted the society like cancer disease. The people involved in the acts of corruption have clearly violated the trust reposed in them by the people, the law and Constitution. The rich and influential people are not ordinary criminals. They are people apart from the common street criminals who snatch away bags and gold chains, pilfer shops and godowns, loot trains and houses, commit murders, kidnap for ransom, indulge in burglary and so on.

As long as we are constrained by a proclivity towards solution of the socio-legal problems, we will remain impotent in addressing the control and management of socio-legal problems. The compilation is a unique treatment of the subject.

However, small a work may be or however big project may become, it is always certain that mistakes do creep in and I am no exception. Any suggestion, criticism from our readers would be most welcome and it shall be our best endeavour in bringing out the next edition of this book.

My thanks goes to my wife Dr. (Mrs) Leena Dutta Bharali for her unstinted support extended to me in compiling the topics of the subject.

Dr. Nalini Kanta Dutta

1

Introduction

The current socio-legal problems are important not only in view of the interaction of a complex cluster of factors, but also because of their implications for the quality of life of individuals and of nations. Most of the articles composed on the issues take stock of the recent trends related to socio-legal problems.

The social and legal problems arising out of dishonesty, misdeeds, partiality in all respects, destruction, violence, greed, crazynees, criminal as well as immoral acts, jealousy, delinquency, selfishness and other falacies of human being causes misery and insecurity to people individually or in groups. Human being desire security—economic, social and legal. Yet almost everywhere their lot in life is insecurity. We are living in the last decades of the turbulent 20th century and about a half decade of 21st century that has seen the gigantic social changes, a profound crisis of morality, ethical behaviour, security and harmony. Such a tragic and indelible mark in the history of the present day society confronted with the development strategies and good conscience of the nations. It is also a fact that a spectacular achievements of social, scientific and technological thoughts opened up before the present and future generations at the cost of acute confrontation between the old and the new, the forces of reaction and the forces of progress. This epoch-making battle is growing in scope and intensity.

Law is the basic need of a State in the processes of emergence, development and functioning in the sectoral disciplines. Sectoral discipline include many areas of scientific and technological innovations and development, sociology, political economy, scientific communication, legal disciplines, history and so on. The problems connected to the fulfillment of the needs and aspirations in the processes of development whether sectoral, state or any area-specific are being created by anti-social elements at various levels.

Personal insecurity, anti development, antisocial activities are generally created by the people with corrupt and criminal mentality, such people are directly connected to crime and politics. We argued that the State, the law and organised society in general can provide only very limited protection against threat to personal security and development of nations in all respects. The State by its very nature is incapable of stamping out crime which it can only contain and control, crime being a basic manifestation of human individuality, whereas illegal politics rising to a challenging reveals the State's own ambiguity and corresponding weakness and vulnerability as order. Similarly the selfish interests of a country may resist advancement of an another country or countries of domination which also may be accounted as socio-legal problem. As for instance, manufacturing nuclear weapons in violation of international treatise, exploration of outer space in violation of international law etc.

Another socio-legal problem connected to personal insecurity and anti-development of a society or nation is crime and delinquency. The State is to assess whether an act done by an individual or a group is lawful or unlawful or invalid or valid. In case of unlawful or invalid act, infringement of law by the State is necessary. Law must be adopted to the needs of the time. Law is necessary to provide ways and means for the living of a good life or to guard the rights and liberties declared by the State. The acts of crime and offences intensified in the present day society. The terrorism and corruption are the major acts of crime and offence of the present day society causing severe destruction of value system. Terrorism is now flourishes, from a regional level to the international level. Today the grains of terrorism has become a part of daily news with the headlines of newspapers smugged with bloom. The worldwide phenomenon of terrorism has unfortunately now come to stay in India. It manifests itself in political, religious and socio-economic inequalities and exploration. It thrives in grievances real or imaginary. So long as terrorism is continue to flourish in the society the nations of the world continue to loose their opportunities for development.

The growing criminalisation of socio-economic life in India is an indicator of degradation of morality and integrity of the population at large. People in power and politics shows the worst record of corruption. Absolute power corrupt absolutely. In a country like India where administration itself is corrupted nothing can be expected for creation of a society free from corruption and demoralisation. The most dangerous phenomenon under the present environment in India is the nexux among politicians, bureaucrates, businessmen and criminals. The nexus is not only very powerful, but quite deadly. Instances like, Hawala Scam, Harshad Mehta Bank Scam, Animal Husbandry Scam of Bihar may be cited against the deadly nexus.

Every criminal in a society whether a white collar criminal or other types of criminal are not concerned with their fellow beings and fails in social interests. It is the duty of the State to provide facilities for living well with full security. The facilities concern with the law of the land, order, punishment to criminals and related issues as conventional windows. I am deeply conscious of the great difficulty of the task attempted here on the current socio-legal problems.

2

Secularism in India and Uniform Civil Code

The preamble of the Indian Constitution has declared that the people of India resolved to constitute India into a Sovereign Democratic Republic and to secure to all her citizens—justice—social, economic and political; liberty of thought, expression, belief, faith and worship, equality of status and of opportunity. Is the new society which we want to create a secular society? Is the Sovereign democratic republic of India a secular state? What are the distinguishing features of Indian secularism as contemplated by our Constitution? Is it possible to create one society and one law as envisaged by the Indian Constitution? Is our society classless and the law uniform? The questions become relevant and important to make India a Socialistic, Democratic country as intended by the framer of the constitution. Secularism by its meaning according to *Encyclopaedia Britanica,* Vol. XX. page-264, is non -spiritual having no concern with religious or spiritual matters. The meaning would show that secularism is distinct, opposed to or not connected with religion or ecclesiastical things. In a commendable and perspective study on the question whether India can be regarded as a Secular State, Donald Engeno Smith repudiated the Indian Secularism being unaccommodative within the definition of secularism which involves three distinct but interrelated sets of relationships concerning the state, religion and the individual. These sets of relations are (1) Religion and individual (Citizenship) (2) The State and the Individual (Citizenship) and (3) The State and Religion (separation of State and Religion).

Regarding the policy of Indian Secularism, it appears that the policy of non-alignment followed by India in foreign affairs is a reflection of the ideal of secularism in her domestic policy. Tyabjee said " I am aware that- its principal architect pandit Jawaharlal Nahru never projected it as such". This was due to the strong antipathy and suspicion that persons like him with agnostic views who have all through their political lives been confronted by opponents with narrow sectarian, communal vies developed against giving religion any recognition in the contents or even formulation of their own political ideology. An examination of the policy adopted by our country reveal that, India can neither wholly succeed in implementing a secular policy at home with simultaneously pursuing a non-aligned Foreign Policy, nor can the foreign policy become really effective unless it is based on a genuinely secular democratic policy. In India the term "Secularism" is interpreted in such a way as if India has no religion. The Constitution of India has not interpreted the doctrine of secularism. It has accepted the doctrine of tolerance of religions and diversity subject to the laws of social control suited to the conditions of India.

India is a multi-lingual and multi-religion state. When India became free the States were not divided on the linguistic basis. The Constitution does not contain any definition of linguistic or religious minorities. The internationally formulated definition of "minority" is the term minority includes only those not dominant groups in a population which possess and wish to preserve stable ethnic, religious or linguistic traditions or characteristics markedly different from those of rest of population (United Nations Sub-Committee on the prevention of discrimination and protection of minorities).

However the concept of secularism introduced and applied in India is not a passive or negative doctrine. It is a comprehensive, forward-looking dynamic doctrine. The declared objective of the Indian Constitution is to create a new social order in which social equality will become a reality and economic justice will prevail. While, endeavouring to achieve this objective, religion may reject its relevance. But, adoption or non-adoption of such relevance of religion makes no difference to the secular society which we want to create in India. Secularism learns on reason rather than on tradition, on experience, rather than on blind faith and it seeks to solve socio-economic problems by debate and dialogue. In a secular state there will be no occasion for communal tension or for conflicts between groups of citizens following different religion. But to achieve the true social objectives of secularism in India which is a multi-religious and multi-lingual country, a Uniform Civil Code for the citizens as a whole irrespective of their religion or language must be introduced to govern and regulate under the same rule or law throughout the country. It is the only solution to the great communal problem. Our Constitution envisages one society and one law. The society is to be classless and law is to be uniform.

India is a land of diversities. Hindus, Muslims, Christians, and other religious groups follow; their own personal laws in family matters which to a great extent differ from one another. Such type of laws instead of serving the purpose of unity and integrity of the country encouraged separatists tendencies which are determined to any growing democracy. Thus keeping in view the traditional interest the fathers of the Constitution by incorporating Article 44 in the Constitution provide for the establishment of Uniform Civil Code to have one law for all the citizens of this country. This Article makes it crystal clear that it is an imperative duty of the state to make efforts in this regard. But it is quite unfortunate to record that on appropriate and effective enactment of legislation by the successive governments of independent India for the establishment of uniform civil code as an obligatory duty is still remain as a crisis. The combination of Art. 44, List III, Entry-5 and Art. 12 of the constitution makes it clear that it is not only the duty of the legislature, but of the each and every functionaries to make efforts towards securing a common code for citizens of this country so that our democracy, which is still in infant stage may grow with the passage of time. The very purpose of our democratic system is to remove all kinds of barriers i.e. religion, caste, creed and to provide with a law which may help to maintain a rule of law in the Indian society. This noble objective envisaged by our Constitution cannot be achieved under the prevailing situations of conflicts amongst religious groups without creating a Uniform Civil Code for all citizens irrespective of religion, caste, creed, language or any other group. Religion must be restricted to spheres which legitimately appertain to religion and the rest of life must be regulated unified and modified in such a manner that we may evolve as early as possible a strong and consolidated nation. While the Constitution guaranteed freedom of religion and conscience, it seeks to divorce religion from personal law and social relations and from laws governing inheritance, succession and marriage just as it has been done in Muslim countries like Egypt and Turkey.

If we look back to the British period, we find that the British government in India also control all citizens and to achieve certainty and uniformity. By passing the Charter Act of 1853 the second Law Commission put forward policies and principles of future codification in India. In 1861 another Law Commission was appointed for the preparation of Draft Code regarding Civil Law in India. On February 11 1879, the Fourth Law Commission WAS appointed with a goal of codifying all the substantial law prevailing in British India. By the efforts of various Law Commissions, criminal laws were codified and the Indian Penal Code, 1861 and Criminal Procedure Code, 1898 came into force and is applicable to all India irrespective of their religion and religious belief. But there was no common civil code. Some other important legislations during British period are (1) The Caste Disabilities Removal Act, 1850 (2) the Indian Contract Act, 1872 (3) The Transfer of Property Act, 1882 (4) The Indian Evidence Act, 1872 (5) The Indian Succession Act, 1865 and (6) the Child Marriage Act, 1928.

After Independence the Indian Government has practically failed to implement the aims and objectives of the Constitutional provisions of Art. 44 and its connected Articles. The contest over the Uniform Civil Code is not something new. But unfortunately this Art. is very often opposed by one section of community or the other. The State instead of making any serious attempt in this direction tends to adopt an indifferent attitude ostensibly as a matter of political expediency. Our government since Independence have not adopted any measure to fight the obscurantists who opposed the uniform civil code. The present government at the centre should take effective steps to overcome the difficulties created in implementing the objective of Art. 44 for the interest of a consolidated Notion in India. The attempt should be made to enact a Uniform Civil Code embodying what is best in all personal laws.

3

Crisis of Morality in Ethical Behaviour

Morality came to be identified as a specific, relatively independent form of social consciousness. The earliest European writings of Homer and Hesiod's poems, the pronouncement of seven wise men of Greece show that the emergence and development of ethical thinking proceeded parallel to the identification of abstract moral norms which were compared with the individuals' behaviour and, as rule it counterposed to it. Ethical intellectualism with its demand for self-restraint provided a way to substantiate and impose on the individual moral standards which were frequently quite alien to him and even contrary to his vital needs. For all civilized societies nothing is more important than re-establishment of morality and justice. While moral regeneration and degeneration is a continuous process in the changing society; but all-round debasement of human values in the post-World War II era has been beyond imagination. The moral crisis between man and himself, man and man, man and nature, and man and State has led to a dangerous situation casting shadow on the conscience, humanity, idealism and other common interests.

The cynical use of money power and political power in India has caused exploitation of the week, poor and backward people, racial and class antagonism, terrorism, fundamentalism, militarism, suppression and repression of human freedom and liberty, all of which have lowered man below human, leading to general lawlessness, unrighteousness and injustice in the society. Although the World War II was fought to establish democracy and to guarantee human liberty and social justice the aftermath of the War has led to erosion of values in all respects leading to lawless law without conscience and concern for man and society. The elite class of the society in particular becomes the example of using the most unscrupulous means to enlarge their already ample fortunes. Their indifference to the injuries and deaths of innocent people due to Government's violation of human rights and the weakness and corruption of the enforcement effort certainly cast our society in a dark light.

Moral values cannot be lost in a civilized society. Increasing criminal activities and lawlessness highlight the prevailing circumstances of moral degradation. Crime has become one of the greatest public concerns of our time. Television, radios and newspapers are filled with shocking accounts of murder and mayhem. Politicians strain to outdo rach other back to the street. But there is a strange distortion in all this, as though the public has lost sight of the real problem and instead, sees only its misshapen reflection. The love of power and pomp encourages politicians to attempt to gain and retain power through corrupt means. The dishonest practices adopted by the political parties and their leaders in the process of election only to gain power and privilege without a sense of moral duties and love for the nation are the root cause of the spread of corruption in the society as a whole. All the ideals of socialism and collective wealth, which seemed to inspire our lawmakers, have been subverted by the misuse of the enormous power placed in the hands of Ministers and officials. This, in turn, accounts for the proliferation of laws whose objective appears to be neither a good administration nor justice. As such the political leaders. Ministers, MPs and MLAs have been maintaining a double standard of morality in society. Thus the elite class has been exploiting the common people, causing a decline in civilization.

The mental complex of the Ministers in general since the formation of independent Government in India has been cultivating a self-centred culture without thinking for their fellow citizens and for the country as a whole. Even Sri Nehru, a man of great integrity himself, had been widely accused of shielding corrupt men through a false sense of loyalty to friends and associates. In the absence of a Code of Conduct for Ministers, MPs and MLAs, the whole objective of democracy has been defeated. The setting up of an Ombudsman type authority has become a public issue ever since July 1959 when Sri CD Deshmukh, then chairman of the University Grants Commission and a former Union Finance Minister raised the issue in the course of a public lecture in Madras. Speaking at Bombay on April 22, 1964, Sri MC Setalvad, former Attorney General of India emphasised the necessity of establishing the institution of Ombudsman in India, particularly in view of the professed goal of a Welfare State. He said that, if democracy in India had to survive, the grievances of the people should be redressed expeditiously and corruption rooted out. Similar opinion had been publicised by many eminent persons thought the years. But, it is a matter of great concern that the successive Governments had not been in favour of creating a code of conduct for Ministers and politicians.

The system of moral regulation in a society plays the part of reference points by which man shapes his behaviour in society. Either overtly or in a disguised form, moral values are reflected everywhere in the spiritual culture of society. It is a consolidated form in the makeup of moral consciousness prevailing under a given social system, in recognised moral codes and people's thoughts and feelings. A society that does not give weight on moral values have to face the consequences of injustice. Strict adherence to a high standard of ethical behaviour is a dire need of the hour.

4

Human Rights and Humanitarian Laws

Human rights have always found a pride of place in the theocracy of religious beliefs of all ages throughout the world. It is indeed, noteworthy that human rights have always had a close link with man's civilization and even today their existence is a symbolic attainment of the standard of civilization. Up to the early part of the 20th century, the neglect of human rights continued by the imperialist of colonial European powers. The freedom of religion was denied and as a result the recognition of human rights by religions existed in different forms was marked with brutality and inhuman practice of depriving human rights which were degenerating. However, the history of civilized societies clearly indicates that, importance was given to human rights. American Declaration of Independence of 1766, the Bill of Rights of 1688 passed by British democrate are the witnesses of recognition of human rights.

The recognition of human rights became absolute when the philosophy generated by the U.N. Charter affirming the dignity of man. The Charter refers to the problem of human rights in its preamble and six different Articles. The words "promoting and encouraging respect for human rights" and "assisting in the realisation of human rights and fundamental freedoms" appears with certain variations in Article-1. The purposes enshrined in Art. 1 of the Charter are (1) to develop friendly relations among nations based on respect for the principles of equal rights and self-determination of people and to take other appropriate measures to strengthen universal peace and (2) to achieve international cooperation in solving international problems of an economic, social, cultural, or humanitarian character and in promoting and encouraging respect for human rights and for fundamental freedoms for all without distinction as to race, sex, language or religion. Other Articles dealing with human rights are Article 13, 55, 56, 62 and 76.

Enlistment, of human rights in the U.N. Charter alone have no impact without its enforcement by legal implication. Law is stated to be a command to be obeyed and hence its due observance is inherent in its very concept. Moral recommendations of human rights without legal link of enforcement have no force. Thus if a law confers a right, there must be a remedy in the event of its violation. The remedy for restoration of rights follows two successive steps first step being the judicial pronouncement. There must be a judicial machinery which applies the law to the facts of a case brought before it and gives a verdict. The second step is its enforcement. The rights unenforceable in character becomes a mereshadow without substance and ceases to be legal right. The basic problems of enforcement of human rights differs at national as well as at international level. Since human rights take their origin within the national arena, look for its survival to the national forum, whether the executive, legislative or the judiciary and rely on national machinery. The international aspect of human rights profounds equally throughout the world irrespective of its extension whether regional, global or universal. Within the framework of international law, there is no provision of compartmentalization of human rights to limited boundaries. The human race is same and one throughout the world and their rights also must necessarily spill over the national limits. So, an international machinery must function to protect human rights of mankind in general. In this respect the international conventions and U.N. resolutions have played a vital role. In addition to the United Nations organisation, all other international Non-governmental organisations such as Amnesty International, Association for the study of the World Refugee Problem, Carnegie Endowment for International peace, commission of the Churces on international Affairs (world Council of Churches), consultative Council of Jewish organisations, International Committee of the Red Cross, world peace Council, international Academy of Human Rights Paris, International Association of Democratic Lawyers etc. strengthened the international machinery for the protection of human rights.

The Problems of Human Rights enforcement differs in peace time and in times of arms conflict, protection of human rights at the time of war becomes acute and this is the most important problem of today as the world facing a freightening race in the amassing a hyper-destructive weapons which could destroy the entire human race As such human rights in armed conflicts involve an international aspect as wars are between two sovereign States, but, the international aspect exists without a tribunal to administer the humanitarian laws of war. Inspite of this serious limitation the enforcement of human rights seems significant owing to the strong factor of reciprocal advantage based on overall self interest coupled with the fear of retaliation and world public opinion. The international control over the manufacture and possession of prohibited weapons of war fare contrary to humanitarian laws in the relevant way to protect human rights during war time. States should manufacture only those weapons of war that are not prohibited by the laws of war. Production of hyper-destructive weapons are capable of indiscriminate annihilation with unknown genetic effects whether based on nuclear device or poisonous gas. So, an effective control on the production of such dangerous weapons is a dire need for the existence not only to entire human race but also to all lives on earth.

Protection of human rights during peace time appears to be followed of a different mechanism. Every State has a duty to treat all persons under its jurisdiction with respect for human rights and fundamental freedoms without distinction as to race, sex language or religion. In racial conflicts as in the case of South Africa the human right violation becomes an acute problem. In 1953 the U. N. General Assembly found that the racial policies of the government of South Africa and their consequences are contrary to the U. N. Charter on human rights. The security council interfered with the racial situation in South Africa for the first time in March/April, 1960, when it called upon South Africa to abandon its policies of apartheid and racial discrimination and requested the Secretary General in consultation with the Government of South Africa to make such arrangements as would adequately help in up- holding the purpose and principles of the Charter. Thereafter the Security Council pursued the matter for protection of human rights in South Africa by different actions.

Protection of human rights is an essential criteria for development "through removal of poverty and exploitation. The subject of citizen's involvement in development operation to legitimise their voices, to convert their articulation into the dominant theoretical paradigm acceptable both to North/ South and East/west was discussed in the International Indira Gandhi Memorial Conference held at New Delhi in 1989. Growth with equality is a major task of all the development planning and as such development has a major responsibility in the protection of human rights.

The basic concept of Indian Constitution is to ensure dignity of man and freedom from want and protection against social, economic and political oppression. Article 14 ensures equality before law to all persons, whether citizens or foreigners, rich or poor, man or woman prime Minister or pauper. Article 14 provides that " the State shall not deny to any person equality before the law or the equal protection of laws within the territory of India". Article 15 and 16 amplify specific aspects of equality before law by declaring that no citizen is discriminated on the ground of religion, race, caste, sex, place of birth, or be subject to any disability, or restriction with regard to access to public places or equal opportunity to public offices. Article 17 is directed towards abolition of untouchability and Article 18 for abolition of title. Article 19 guaranteed seven freedoms to citizens. Article 20 protects every individual against ex post facto (retrospective) criminal law, double jeopardy and testimonial compulsion. Article 21 of the Constitution provides that no person shall be deprived of his life or personal liberty or life of a citizen except in accordance with law and procedure established by law. In addition to such rights some other rights are also guaranteed by the Indian Constitution. These are right to freedom of religion (Art. 25 to 28), Cultural and Educational rights (Art. 29 and 30). But, the provisions of such rights to the citizens and non-citizens alone will be illusory in nature unless effective remedies for enforcement are provided.

Observance of human rights in peace time conferred on nation States and rely basically on the organs of the Sovereign State for enforcement of their rights. This reliance must be on judicial organs having independence of judiciary.

In general all States in the world do not violate human rights in peace time and thereby no threat to humanity as a whole. But a few States do not generally respect human rights in peace time. Building up of world public opinion against the defaulting States is necessarily a relevant factor for human rights enforcement. Human rights in armed conflicts are governed by International law. The force of humanitarian laws as an international aspect rests on treaties and declarations. So, this is the time we tempted to look forward to the force vigours created through International Conventions against violation of human rights particularly in arms conflict.

5

Preventive Detention Laws: Its Use and Misuse

The "Preventive Detention" as the term in use to prevent continuing activities of somebody which are prejudicial to the maintenance of public order has not defined under Indian law. The justification of each detention as described in the Acts is on suspicion or reasonable probability of the detenu committing an act likely to cause harm to the society or endanger the security of the state. Though the laws of preventive detention is fundamentally different from imprisonment after trial and conviction in a criminal court, these laws are repugnant to democratic constitution and as such no democratic countries like the U.S.A., the U.K etc., intend to incorporate such laws into their constitutional framework. The constitution of India recognises preventive detention even in normal times.

The first preventive detention Act in India was enacted by the parliament on 26th February, 1950. The object of the Act was to provide for detention with a view to preventing any person from acting in a manner prejudicial to the defence and relation of India with foreign powers as well as the security of India or a State or the maintenance of the public order.

The Preventive Detention Act of 1950 was allowed to

lapse on 31st December 1969. However after a brief gap of about two years, the preventive Detention laws was revived again in the form of maintenance of Internal security Act, (MISA) 1971 and remained in operation till it was repealed in 1978. The subject of the Act dealt with was not new in the field of legislation in India. The forerunners of the Act have been the Preventive Detention Act of 1950. Its amendments and the various enactments of the State Legislatures which bore provisions identical to these of the enactment of MISA. Though the expression Preventive Detention has not been defined in the Acts, nor anywhere in Indian law, it is to be understood that as used in contradiction to the expansion "Preventive Detention". Detention to such form during peace time was foreign to any civilized form of government. Such measures were adopted in England for the first time during the World War I. At the outbreak of the war, Defence of the realm Consolidated Act of 1914 was passed, providing for preventive detention and it ceased to have effect at the ceasation of hostilities. It was re-enacted at the initiation of the World War-II. Preventive detention measures in England, therefore had all along been regarded as purely war measures. In India though the regulations similar to English ones framed at the advent of the war under the defence of India Act, continued to remain in the Statute books even after the war. It is therefore surprising to note that the representatives of the free people in independent India elected to elevate the status of preventive detention measures by making it an integral part of the Constitution. Preventive Detention finds mention in List-I as well as in List-III under the seventh schedule (Article 246) to the Constitution. Entry 9 of List-I (Union List) provide for making of laws on "Preventive Detention" for reasons connected with defence, Foreign affairs or the Security of India. Entry 3 of List-III (Concurrent List) empowers the

Central and State Legislature to make laws on preventive detention for reasons connected with the Security of the State the maintenance of public order or the maintenance of supply and services essential to the community. However, the law making powers of Legislature conferred under these provisions are not absolute. In making legislation, the Fundamental Rights guaranteed to the citizen of India in Part-III under Article 13(2) of the Constitution have to be respected and unless otherwise saved by the provisions of the Constitution, they will be void to the extent they contravene the provisions of part-III. Under Art, 245(1). the legislative power conferred under Art 246 is also made subject to the provisions of this Constitution which of course include part-III dealing with fundamental Rights. The relevant provisions under the heading of Fundamental Rights for the purpose of preventive Detention or similar Acts are Art, 21 and Art, 22.

Even since 1950 the centre had preventive detention except for brief gaps for two times between January 1971 and then from March 1977 till October 1980. The National Security Ordnance Promulgated on 22 September, 1980 for preventive detention of persons responsible for communal disharmony, extremist activities and for a number of other activities prejudicial to maintenance of security of the country. This ordinance was repealed by the National Security Act, 1980 (NSA) on 27th December, 1980. NSA is the prevailing law on the preventive Detention. The validity of NSA, 1980 was challenged from time to time in a good number of cases. In A.K. Roy Vs. Union of India (AIR, 1982, SC 710) the Supreme Court while upholding the constitutional validity of the Act, observed that various provisions of NSA are not either directly or indirectly violative of the provisions of Article 19, 21 and 22 of the constitution of India.

The salient feature of NSA is that in order of preventive detention can be made by the central and the State government if it is satisfied with respect to any person that it is necessary to do so to prevent him from acting in any manner prejudicial to the defence of India, the relations of India with foreign persons, security of India, security of State, maintenance of public order or the maintenance of supplies and services essential to the community. In the case of Ram Monohor Lohia Vs. State of Bihar, AIR, 1966, SC 740, Hidayatullah, then justice of the Supreme Court considered the concept of "Law and order" public order and the security of the state which are generally used in the preventive detention law and indicated that to appreciate the extent and scope of one of them would have three concentric circles, the largest of them representing public order and lastly security of the State. Preventive detention is a serious invasion of personal liberty.

Another preventive detention law in the name of "The Conservation of foreign Exchange and Prevention of smuggling Activities Act (COFEPCSA) was promulgated in India on 13th December, 1974. This Act has been provided to replace the Amendment made in the maintenance of Internal Security Act by a separate independent status. An order under the Act can be passed if the authority is satisfied that it is necessary to prevent a person from (a) smuggling goods or (b) abetting the smuggling goods or (c) smuggling in transporting or concealing keeping smuggled goods or (d) dealing in snuggled goods otherwise then by engaging in to importing or concealing or keeping smuggled seeds or (c) harbouring persons engaged in smuggling goods to betting the smuggling of goods. The Act continued remain in inforce during Janata Regins eventhough the maintenance of internal security Act. 1971 was repealed by the government.

At the end of the Janata Regime (I) Government headed by Mrs. Indira Gandhi returned to power another preventive detention Act namely "prevention of Black Marketing and maintenance of Supplies of Essential Commodities Act, 1980 (PBMSECA) was enacted as the first Act relating to the preventive Detention law by the parliament. The Act authorised the Central and State government to make an order detaining a person with a view to preventing him from committing black marketing and from acting in any manner prejudicial to the maintenance of supply of commodities essential to the community.

The object of preventive detention suggests that the condition of such detention should not be punitive in nature. Our Constitution provides protection and safeguards of the rights of citizens under Article 21 and 22. Article 21 of the Constitution lays down that "No person shall be deprived of his life and liberty except according to procedure established by law" Similarly Art. 22 prescribed safeguard to the citizen which should not be violated or ignored by the State authorities while exercising its power of preventive detention to detain a person. The desired safeguards like periodical review of detention cases issue of speaking order by the government or Advisory Board, impaling Constitutional obligation on parliament to prescribe the maximum period of detention providing legal assistance to the detenues etc. will curtail or minimise the injustices done to a detenu. Until and unless the government at the centre is careful in introducing and implementing the preventive detention laws so as to preserve the rights and personal liberties of the detenu within the framework of the Indian Constitution it will be difficult to create a congenial atmosphere.

6

Narcotic Drugs: Their Use and Abuse

Narcotic drugs include opium and various derivatives thereof, such as morphine, heroin and codeine; mandrax, coca leaves and their derivatives such as coccaine. Opium is the dried milky exudate obtained from the unripe seed pods of the poppy plant which grows extensively in Turkey, India, Pakistan, Iran, Nepal, Yugoslavia and Bulgaria. In India, poppy for opium is cultivated under strict government supervision in Madhya Pradesh, Rajasthan and UP. The processing plants in Gazipur (UP) and Neemach (MP) were set up by the British in 1820. Heroin, opium and morphine are derived from the same source, the poppy plant. The addictive substances contained in narcotic drugs are called alkaloids. Of the 20 or more alkaloids found in opium, only a few are used for production of medicine. References on the use of narcotic drugs are available in records of history from the time of Mesopotomia (5000 to 4000 BC).' Homer's writings indicate Greek usage of the substance at least by 900 BC. Mention of the use of addicted substances either as medicine or stimulants are found in religious epics of ancient time.

In the early part of 19th century, opium because somewhat of a medical panacea and a variety of patent medicines made of opium were available in the West. They were used by all social classes. The invention of the hypodermic needle in the mid 19th century was the subsequent development of its use as medicine. Towards the end of 19th century, various undesirable elements such as gamblers and prostitutes began to be associated with the use of opium and narcotics and became identified more with the criminal elements than with medical therapy. By the turn of the 20th century, narcotic use had become a worldwide problem. Under the prevailing situation, national and international regulatory bodies become a dire need to control traffic in opium from the near "and Far East. The problem started at the beginning with the poor and culturally deprived class of people. But, nowadays, indiscriminate use and abuse of narcotic drugs by all classes of people become a common practice and thereby create a critical problem in the society. Presently the student community in particular is being widely involved in drug addiction. Thousands of people in the western world are dying every year because they have become dependent on drugs. In New York alone in three years 3000 died from overdosing themselves with narcotics. Cigarette smoking kills hundreds of thousands each year either through various cancers or heart disease. The figures of drug addiction and death cases might go up recently in India also. The lives of many families are made intolerable because of either alcohol or drug dependence of one or more members. Under the prevailing instability of the societies, more and more people, especially youngsters turn to drugs for escape from the pressures of living. At first many school children simply take a puff of a drug-filled cigarette, out of curiosity or simply to keep up with others. For most that is as far as it goes, but for a few, it is the first step to drug addiction. Within a few years, smoking marijuana has led to using harder drugs, often to injecting heroin into the body which usually ends with death. At the least, drug addiction causes mental disturbance or damages the nervous system and because drugs are expensive to buy, addicts often have to resort to crimes to get the money they need. The problem today is made worse by the high rate of unemployment. The youngsters are easy prey for the street corner dealers who sell small packets of heroin. Narcotics induce the youngsters, a sense of euphoria, a release from the worry of trying to cope with life. Once an addict has started maintaining, he or she will need upto two grams a day to satisfy the craving and will eventually go to any length to get it.

Nowadays the problem of drug addiction has become widespread and critical enough to control it effectively. Customs Officers and narcotic agents have found it almost impossible to stop the flow of drugs into different parts of the world. The sources of their supply are so plenty that seizing of huge quantities of narcotics by Customs Officers cannot reduce the flow to even a small extent. Massive efforts have so far made by international conventions for suppressing the contraband traffic and the abuse of dangerous drugs. But, the problem instead of reducing, is aggravating day by day. India is a state signatory to the Geneva Convention. India also participated in the second International Opium Conference convened in accordance with the resolution of the Assembly of the League of Nations met at Geneva in 1924 and adopted the convention relating to dangerous drugs. Since then the Government of India is constantly associated with control measures in various ways. But, it is unfortunate to record that, India instead of becoming free from drugs traffic, developed into a fairly big base for the narcotic trades. Morphine and heroin began to be promoted by organised gangs which operated from the Golden Cresent and Golden Triangle. The failure of the government to eradicate the problem is due to operation of outdated laws and corruption in implementation of the existing laws. Smugglers involved in the trade were being released on bail for petty amounts and quite a few jumped bail. Those convicted under trial received minor punishments. The insurgencies developed in the North-East have created drug smugglers in huge numbers and the government has practically no control over it. Every drug dealer in the country probably knows that even if he is arrested for selling drugs, he will not to prison. In 1985, drug abuses had began to assume alarming proportions in Madras city's schools and colleges and suddenly declined in 1986. One reasons for the decline is attributed to heroin's sudden security. The police traced its disappearance to the fact that SRI, Lanka Tamil refugees, who were the major peddlers, have been slowly going back to Jaffa. In the concern region, drug abuse become intense due to active involvement of the Naga and Mizo rebels taking advantage of its passage through Barma and other neighbouring countries. The Narcotic Drugs and Psycho tropic substances Act, 1986, if implemented properly, like the conviction of a youth from Madhya Pradesh in 1986, to a term of ten years rigorous imprisonment and a fine of rupees one lakh the drug abuse's definitely be deterred to a desirable extent. Many suggestions have been made from various corners to render the law enforcement machinery more efficient. The growing corruption within the ranks of law enforcement machinery must be curbed. The mobility of law enforcement officials should be improved by equipping them with modern scientific, technical and specialised knowledge. More arrests more convictions, longer sentences, more seizures of drug dealers assets are necessary to check the growing menace of narcotic traffic and drug and be stopped at source through National and international efforts.

7

Drug Addiction: A Serious Concern of the Youths

Drug addiction results in physical and mental deterioration, loss of economic efficiency, degradation of social status, and declination of associates with consequences of euphorism and hallucination. Drugs which call forth physical dependence and tolerance very easily lead to chronic abuse with serious consequences. With some of the drugs it is relatively easy to break the habit with several others, however even a short period of use may create a physical dependence that brings about painful withdrawal symptoms. In such cases it is very difficult or impossible to break the habit except during periods when the addict is physically restrained.

Narcotic drugs include opium and the various derivatives thereof such as morphine, heroin and codeine; mundrax, cocoa leaves and their derivatives such as cocaine. The use of euphoric and stimulating drugs has been known throughout history among most people. According to available reports, there are about 150,000 heroin addicts in Bombay, another 100000 in Delhi and between 60,000 to 70,000 in Calcutta and at present the users of drugs increasing cumulatively and spreading rapidly in all the States in India including Assam posing a serious problem of the society. If the present trends continue there would be about 15 million drug addicts in the country at the turn of the century as predicted by some experts at a seminar held in Calcutta in 1986. The present wave of drug addiction has overtaken almost all countries around the world. The intensity of addiction varies from country to country due to varying capabilities of its control. Drug addiction cases in India alarmingly increased during last five years. Earlier it was a problem of affluent youngsters and the urban elite. For most of them it was a, status symbol. To-day it extends to poor and illiterate masses. The persistent problem of drug addiction now threatens to strangle the student community in India mostly in cities, towns. Universities colleges, schools and hostels of educational Institutions. Drug users are now available even in villages. As such drug abuse has taken on a new aspect as it has also become Intimately connected with the new youth culture. Among chronic abusers, there are some who are severely damaged by the drugs, particularly amphetamine, which is often dissolved and injected directly into the veins. Drug abuse among juveniles is typically a group phenomenon. Drug addiction has gripped a sizeable part of our citizens of both sexes and it is most shocking to know that bright school and college boys and girls becoming drug addicts.

Under the diversified sphere of circumstances of the problem of drug addiction, it becomes an exigency to protect the boys and girls from entrapment of drug use at any cost. It is no doubt true that the sickness of government machineries, unconsciousness and indifferent attitude of the public in general are responsible for such drug menaces of the country. The nexus between the police and drug peddlers, drug agents, sub-agents and dealers have boosted up the trade in an extensive scale only to have economic gain at the cost of destruction of lives and properties. Parents prefer to keep it a secret and make little effort for rehabilitation causing absence of corrective facilities. Both government and social control of drug addiction and intoxication with a united effort is a dire need to prevent damages of lives and properties. Enactment of the Opium Act of 1876 (Act I of 1878), the Dangerous Drugs Act of 1930 (Act. 2 of 1930), the Drugs and Cosmetic Act of 1940 and the Drugs (Control) Act of 1950 were steps in the direction of suppressing the contraband traffic and the abuse of dangerous drugs. The deterrent laws created so far in India have practically failed to curb drug menaces for a variety of reasons. The repealed section 82 of the Narcotic Drugs and Psycotropic Substances Act passed by Parliament which came into force with effect from 14th November, 1985 is a stringent provision for the control and regulation of narcotic drugs and psychotropic substances. The new law, no doubt is an improvement over the old but will have little impact on drug merchants, who do not carry or sell drugs themselves. For successful detection it is necessary to collect adequate intelligence not only about the agents and sub-agents but also big operators who do not physically possess narcotics. Corruption amongst law enforcement machineries also creates problem in controlling drug menaces effectively. Nowadays drug smugglers all over the country becomes active in trafficking drugs for easy monetary gains. Increase in the illegal operation of drugs in India has a special significance because of her geographical location. Two important routes of the drug trafficking are placed in India. More than half of the heroin used throughout the world comes from the Golden Triangle where the borders of Burma, Laos and Thailand meet. According to a recent information, drugs are first sent to India from the Golden Triangle and then to the U.S.A. and European countries. Immediately after entering India, drugs are brought to important cities like, Bombay, Calcutta, Delhi and Madras. From these cities drugs are carried by smuggler and sub-agents to other states in

India. It is reported that when ships reach near the ports, the packets of narcotics are thrown into sea, and picked up by small fishing boats. In addition Narcotic drugs are also brought into India from Pakistan, Nepal and Bangladesh. The drugs can be easily smuggled into India through the open Indo-Nepal border from Nepal, through Punjab, Rajasthan, Jammu and Kashmir and Gujarat from Pakistan, through West Bengal and North-Eastern states from Bangladesh and through North-Eastern states from China and Burma. The Golden Cresent route through Delhi and Bombay is particularly well established. With a view to financing Khalistan, Naga, Mizo and TNV underground activists for increasing continuance of terrorist and disruptive activities, Pakistan and other neighbouring countries are encouraging smuggling of Narcotic drugs into India.

Various techniques of trafficking drugs by smugglers are used. Drugs are mostly taken in tiffed suitcases, inside fruits, hollowed cricket bats, walls of refrigerators, implied interiors of dead bodies in the coffin etc. On the Thailand-Malayasia border, freshly murdered babies were cleaned up internally stiffed with heroin and came across by young mothers holding babies. Unless an intensive, all-out effort at all levels are made to uproot not only the regular haunts, dens, peddlers and pushers, who are themselves addicts as well as traders, stockists and financiers the problem will continue to prevail and developed as well. Next to preventive measures, thought should be given for the treatment and rehabilitation of those who are already addicted. During recent years narcotics have become a great menace in Indian society. It has broken many happy homes and families, caused health hazards and criminal behaviour to drug addicts. So, public demand should be grown vigorously not only for efficient preventive measures, but also for treatment of addicts with required facilities.

8

Juvenile Delinquency: Causes and Remedies

> "Persons are selected for criminal conviction not by reference to their moral character or social dangerousness but by reference to their poverty or their helplessness".
>
> —***Francis A. Alien***

The causes of juvenile delinquency may be regarded as (1) Environmental or (2) personal that is physiological or psychological. In developing countries like India, an affluent society brings pressure on young people to spend freely and those who self control and restraint take criminality to satisfy their ever-increasing want. Ever-increasing dishonesty and corruption in high placed leads to such type of influence on young people. They are confronted with a world without morals. The impact of western civilization and temptation for luxuries and pompous life has greatly disturbed the modern youths with the result of a considerable growth in crimes committed by juveniles. As the child grows into adulthood his emotional strivings rooted in the biological structure of man, and are always influenced by environment. His emotions are coloured, consciously or unconsciously, by his biological experiences in childhood. Our personality structure does not exist in us from the first moment we breathe. It is developed in us through our conduct with those with whom we live in infancy and childhood. Any child wherever he is can only watch and initiate those around him. He learns in great haste, from his impressions of his immediate surroundings. A child's desires are originally tied up with biological needs, which if satisfied lead to pleasure, and if dissatisfied lead to pain. The conscious or unconscious goal of every human being to obtain pleasure and to avoid pain is determined by his emotional striving.

Sociologist emphasize the role of the social environment in the etiology, or causes of delinquent behaviour. The major characteristics of societies with high rates of juvenile misconduct are modernisation, urbanisation and industrialisation. Temptation for modern luxuries of life motivate young stars to resort to wrongful acts to satisfy their wants. The industrial development in India has resulted into urbanisation which in twin has given rise to new problems such as, housing slum dwelling, overcrowding, lack of parental control and disintegration and so on. The high cost of living in urban areas makes it necessary even for women to take up outdoor jobs for supporting their family financially. The children of those job-holders left all alone at homes without any parental control. All these factors cumulatively lead to an enormous increase in juvenile delinquency in urban areas.

The family has been called the basis of society. Family environment is of great importance to children because, it is their first society. The family can bring out positive and constructive or negative and destructive traits, depending upon its inner atmosphere. To a large extent the family environment determines whether we express love and affection or hostility and hatred. Undesirable conditions at home, particularly quarrels between parents, desertion, intoxication, immorality of the parent, poverty and lack of employment, overcrowding in one-room-lodging, lack of proper sanitation or conveniences, cruelty of step parent, desertion and lack of care in the case of an unwanted child are the main harmful environment of family life causing children to delinquent to a great extent.

The atmosphere for children at home must be congenial to their good education and well being. The disintegration of family system and laxity in parental control over children is an important cause of increase in juvenile delinquency. Unappropriate rise in divorce cases and matrimonial disputes has also been a vital cause for disrupting family solidarity. Undue discrimination among children or stepmotherly treatment also has an adverse psychological effect on children. The children under no circumstances should be neglected. Negligence of children furnishes a soothing ground for juvenile delinquency. The parents and other elderly members of the family must provide adequate opportunities for their young stars to develop their personality through proper education and training. Coldness on the part of a parent towards the child results in coldness from the child also and not only coldness hut disdain from the child. Dr. K.R. Masani, an eminent psychologist, in his lecture at the 'Silverfish' on 21st June, 1950, related how a child who was brought to him by his mother for rudenss and disdain to her. At play, in Dr. Masani's therapy, the child turned playing with toy dogs--black as also white. The child arranged a big black dog and a big white dog and two small dogs together and then with a rubber ball played the game of throwing down the dogs. Dr. Masani found the child throwing down the white dog far more than the other dogs. In reply, the child explained that the white dog was his mother, the black dog his father and the small dogs were his brother, and sister. Asked why he treated the white dog, i.e. his mother, so roughly and scornfully, the child replied that often he has asked his mother whether she loved him. His mother replied, "I can love you only if you behave well and be a good boy". Though questioned by the child time and again, she sternly replied conditionally as before in her phraseology—most detestable to the child who was pining for his mother's genuine and unconditional love. When he got rejected by his mother's conditional replies, he concluded that his mother had really no love for him. That was the cause of his scornful behaviour towards his mother who really did not know how to behave towards her child.

Intoxication, resulting in assaults on the wife and children and in impoverishment of the whole family, leads to disgusting atmosphere at home so that the children think it best to leave home and seek their own elsewhere, or may take to thieving, failure to earn a living outside the home may lead to the commission of theft. Other causes of juvenile delinquency are (1) bad company (2) adolescent instability and impulses (3) early sex experiences (4) mental conflicts (5) extreme social suggestibility (6) love of adventure (7) motion pictures (8) school dissatisfaction (9) poor recreation (10) street life (11) vocational dissatisfaction (12) sudden impulse and (13) physical conditions of all sorts.

Places such as gambling houses, houses of ill-fame, billiard halls, may corrupt the child or the young person and pave the way to delinquency. Parents should protect their children from such places. Bad cinema shows and dances should be scrupulously avoided. The thwarting of the individuality of the child and the repressior of his just or legitimate desires also cause conflict and often lead to delinquency. To avoid such delinquency, the child should be allowed individuality and just expression of his legitimate desires. Preventive measures such as education, should be adopted. Adult education is of no substantial purpose or use if it does not teach the people the art of proper living. Lack of education at home and at school is a cause of juvenile delinquency. The education which a child receives at home is even more important than that at school, because it is at home that careful and wise parents can notice the defect in their children and get the same removed at any early stage. The teachers in schools must be really efficient; they must, above all be capable of impressing the students under their care and they should see and satisfy themselves that those under their care and guidance have really had their character well developed as to ensure their being let alone in safety on the stage of life.

9

An Effective Juvenile Legislation: Need of the Hour

The most critical problem of the present day society is the economy. Next to the economy our major social problem and most potent source of fear is the juvenile crime. Most of the juvenile criminals become harden and habitual criminal in the later stages of their lives. The other name of juvenile criminal is juvenile delinquent, juvenile delinquency is a world-wide problem and there are deep rooted causes for this problem. The delinquent had become the demon of the twentieth century. A child situated in his family centre tends to be loving to the parents and relative. But there are social and economic factors, deep rooted psychological disturbances which tend to make him unnatural. An effective juvenile legislation based on a thorough study of the problem of juvenile delinquency will certainly go a long way in removing the causes of this malady thus helping in bringing back the delinquent to normalcy. Article 15(3) of the constitution of India empowers the State to make any special provision for women and children. The implication of this provision can be depicted by introducing section 407 of Criminal Procedure Code which prohibits release of a person accused of a capital offence on bail except a woman, a child under sixteen years of age or a sick man has been held valid as meting out a special treatment consistent with Article 15(3).

Juvenile delinquency involves wrong doing by a young person or a child who is under an age specified by the law of the place concerned. A statute may include in the definition of a delinquent child even a "wayward, incorrigible or habitually disobedient child." A child or a young person growing up idly or living in crime or associating with thieves, robbers or bad characters, vagrants prostitutes or vicious persons or a child who visits a gambling saloon or billiard room or wanders about streets at night or who absent himself from home without the consent of parent or guardian may be regarded as a delinquent child. Even a child found homeless or without visible subsistence can be brought up before a juvenile court and dealt with by way of a protective and preventive measure. The causes of juvenile delinquency may be (1) environmental or (2) personal i.e. psychological or physiological. The environmental causes include undesirable conditions at home, particularly quarrels between parents, desertion, intoxication, immorality of the parent poverty and lack of employment, over-crowding in one room-lodging lack of proper sanitation or conveniences, cruelty of step-parent, desertion of lack of care in the case of an unwanted child. Severe discipline at home or at school creates tendency to the child to escape from the environment. A broken home resulting from divorce between the parents or desertion by a parent or death or imprisonment of a parent is an another environmental cause of juvenile delinquency.

The individual causes of juvenile delinquency relates to a number of psychological and physiological conditions of the child or adult. The physical conditions which are responsible for delinquency are--ailments of occular, nose and throat, ear, speech defects, neurosis, phymosis, physical irritations, headaches, overdevelopment in adolescence, hypoglycemia, hypersexualism etc. The psychological conditions causing juvenile delinquency are neurosis and psychosis. The neurotic illness comprise largely of patients with historical conversion or dissociation type of disorder, obsessive compulsive states and anxiety states. The psychoses or insanities are more fruitful cause of criminal behaviour. The common of these illness is depression, a patient who under the effect may commit crime even murder.

Man inherits and learns from environment and by imitation of what others do for good or for evil. According to the sociological school, criminal behaviour is caused in the same way as social behaviour is caused. Unfavourable social conditions may be responsible for criminality, very often the children of parents who smokes are also smokes. This is due to imitation as the child often imitates the parents and form their habits. Very often parents exhibit faulty habits which their children carry by imitation. The use of tobacco and cigarette by children or adults may cause delinquency. The one of tobacco, cigarette or may other toxic substance soon causes an unstable nervous system and way lead to delinquency. In Bengal, there is an Act preventing the use of tobacco by young persons. In Bombay a police officer can prevent a young person or a juvenile smoking on the public road or in a street. An important and very beneficial Act of the Bengal legislation is the Juvenile Smoking Act, 1919. Sec. 3 of that Act prohibits any sale or giving of tobacco or cigarette papers to any young person under the age of sixteen. Section 4 of the Act empowers any Police officer in uniform or any other persons or class of persons duly authorised by the State government to seize any tobacco, pipes or cigarette papers in the possession of any person appearing to be under the age of sixteen years, if he finds him smoking in any street or public place and to destroy may such articles. In Maharashtra and Gujarat by virtue of Section 10(c) of the Bombay Children Act, it is obligatory on a police officer to seize any cigarette, tobacco or any smoking material or instrument found in the possession of any child found smoking in any public place or street. Some other legislative measures on this area undertaken in our country are--(a) Karnataka provision of Juvenile Court Smoking Act, 1911 (b) Punjab Juvenile Smoking Act, 1918 (c) Rajasthan provision of Juvenile Smoking Act, 1950. It is an established fact that smoking at the child age is a pre-delinquency act and as such the legislative measures authorise the court to punish any person who sales or attempt to sale excepting under written order of the parent or guardian or his employer to a person under sixteen years any tobacco or its product. The States who have not yet formed up such Acts should emulate the examples of Bengal, Maharashtra and Gujarat. Parents and guardians should also learn to be wise and see that their children do not smoke and do not use any toxic substances.

The problem of juvenile delinquency is one that concern society's interest. For the delinquent child of today may become the formidable criminal of tomorrow. So, early detection and treatment are necessary, but what is more, we should work for the prevention of crime. Cultural and Psychological education is the most potent in that direction.

The object of juvenile legislation in to protect the children and not to punish. For the benefit and better handling of Juvenile delinquents Acts of the Legislature were passed. Children's and sociotics, Homes, Certified schools (Approved centres) and institution came into existence. A sympathetic handling of juvenile delinquents prevent their growing into daring criminal. At present a good number of children

Acts working in different States in India, the important Acts, being (1) The Bombay Children Act, 1948 (Applied to Maharashtra and Gujarat) (2) Bombay Borstol Schools Act, 1929 (3) The West Bengal Children Act, 1959 (4) The Madras Children Act (5) The Hyderabad Children Act, 1951 (6) The Assam Children Act, 1969 (7) The Bihar Children Act, 1969 (8) The Mysore Children Act, 1964 ((9) The Orissa Reformatory Schools Act, 1897 (10) The U.P. Children Act, 1951 (11) The Children Act, 1960 (applicable to Union Territories).

Sufficient legislations in India so far affected in the States' to deal with juvenile delinquents for the benefit and better handling so as not to breed criminals in the society. But, the most effective requirement for the successful working of children Acts is the proper and whole-hearted, implementation of their provisions which should not be kept in the shelf or merely left in black and white to decorate the statute books. The community must make a sincere attempt if it wants to reduce delinquency and to protect children. Children should be dealt with exclusively by the juvenile courts. The ordinary criminal courts should not have any right of hearing children's cases. A special Juvenile Police Unit with officers well-trained in criminology and with social sympathies, particularly trained women police officers is essential in all the States.

If delinquency symptoms of a child cannot be projected timely and accurately, the criminality develops like any other health and psychic hazards due to various socio-phenomenological and economic reasons. In this respect the parents or guardians have a pivotal duty to take necessary care to check the delinquency may proper institutional care and therapeutic and reformatory justice alike to all delinquent children are most helpful to check

the delinquency from converting to criminal. Similarly, non-formal and non-State authorities are to be recognised and reformed in such a manner that this local authorities can also contribute to the success of the system.

10

Corruption: A Serious Concern of the Masses

In the widest connection corruption includes improper or selfish exercise of power and influence attached to a public life. Securing some kind of material advantage directly or indirectly for oneself or family relative or friends constitutes the most common form of corruption. With the ever-increasing complexities of life in modern time, varied forms of corruption are being practised by dishonest elements in society with a view to acquiring wealth by dubious means. In law corruption is a criminal misconduct. We have had innumerable commissions of enquiry on corruption, lot of amendment of laws to control corruption in addition to which the set-up of police establishment and vigilance units in administration departments and Public Accounts Committee to look after corruption. We have all the laws including Government service conduct rules to combat corruption. But in reality it is very difficult to succeed in reducing such offences.

Corruption may be classified in five categories.

(i) Habitual acceptance of illegal gratification.

(ii) Habitual acceptance of valuable thing without consideration.

(iii) Dishonest or fraudulent misappropriation of property.

(iv) Abuse of official position to obtain a valuable thing.

(v) Possession of property disproportionate to know sources of income.

Attempt to deal with corrupt elements through administration of laws are part of the broader system of social control dedicated to find out a proper balance between individual impulse and the social discipline maintaining the cooperative arrangements known as society. Corruption was existed in the pre-Independence era also in some form or other. After independence the old bureaucratic framework retained. The reason for this is that we were accustomed to this type of administration. The law makers in the United Kingdom laid down under the Government Act, 1933(3 and 4 will IV, C 85) the seeds of Indianisation of the civil services in our country 150 years ago. Although the I.C.S. ceased to function as a service of Secretary of State for India after the 15th August, 1947, when the Indian Independence Act, 1947 was enforced, its members were automatically appointed to corresponding posts under the Crown in condition with the affairs of the Dominion of India or of a province by virtue of the provisions of Sub-clause (i) of clause 7 of the Indian Provisional Constitution Order, 1947. On the other hand the Indian Administrative Service has been created in the same pattern. It was designed to maintain law and order and collect revenue. The British System of administration is actually not suitable to the needs of a developing economy. The senior officials are heavily burdened with additional work with consequential slackness in the degree of supervision. Delays are a regular feature. When great deal of power is concentrated in the hands of low paid staff and the public is ready to offer bribes to expedite their work or obtain undue favours, corruption is bound to flourish. In the process of development after independence so as to make good the time lost over the last two countries, there has come about a certain amount of weakening of the old system of values without its being replaced by effective new values. With the weakening of the social modes of the simples society, signs of materialism and importance of status resulting possession of money and economic power are clearly visible. The post-war overflow of money as a result of war-time controls and scarcities leads to a unhealthy climate for integrity and unprecedented opportunities to the dishonest elements in society of acquiring wealth by dubious means.

In the past the people of India have been crushed by invaders. In the Independent India the people came to tolerate corruption as a normal feature of public life. The unconscious sanction of corruption at various levels is the outcome of some important factors out of which rise of the get-rich-quick politicians, earning as of money and wealth by dishonest employees of Govt., Sami-Govt. and private organisations and high taxation leading to temptation to bribe or to take bribes are prominent. In June, 1962, the Government of India constituted a Committee on prevention of corruption, headed by K. Santhanam, M.P. In its unanimous report the Committee found that the ultimate sources of corruption were (i) Ministers (ii) legislators (iii) political parties and (iv) industrialists and merchants who seeks favours from these three. The fall in integrity among ministers is not uncommon. Some have enriched themselves illegitimately, obtained good jobs for their sons and relations through nepotism. But the Committees recommendations regarding these ultimate sources of corruption have not received serious attention. Black money earned by concealing income for the purpose of tax evasion is growing at a fast rate. According to the findings of IMF, the quantum of black money in India at present will be about 50 per cent of GNP and generating at the rate of Rs. 2 crores per hour. Prof. Kaldor in his report on Indian Tax Reform submitted to the Government of India in 1953-54 estimated that the amount of black money was of the order of Rs. 600 crores or 6 per cent of GNP at market prices. In the sixtees the Government instituted the Direct Tax Enquiry Committee (DTEC) popularly known as the Wanchoo Committee, to have a fresh look at the matter. This Committee mainly adopted the methodology of Kaldor and later submitted its report in 1971. According to DTEC, the amount of black money generated in 1968-69 was of the order of Rs. 1400 crores (4.2% of GNP). Another major cause of corruption in India is the use of black money in election by the political parties. The coiling on election expenses for a Lok Sabha seat is Rs.1 lakh, while for a State Assembly seat is Rs. 50,000, B.K. Nehru a seasoned bureaucrat and Ex-Governor of Jammu and Kashmir, said in a public lecture in 1980: "It was estimated that the cost of an election in a Parliamentary Constituency was Rs. 5 lakhs to Rs. 20 lakhs and that in a State Assembly Constituency between Rs. one lakh and Rs. 5 lakhs. There were 542 elected members to Lok Sabha and 3533 members of State Assemblies. The total seat to the parties and the candidates was colossal. The system has tended to generate into a more direct relationship between the money contributed and the favour granted. Once this nexus was accepted as a valid commitment of the democratic culture, not even the most powerful leader could stop the advance of corruption. Those who entered politics were not men interested in policy. A large number of them would be hard put to it to enunciate what the election manifestos of their respective parties contain. They were in legislatures in the persuit of power. In one particular State not less than 30 par cent of the legislatures were involved in criminal cases. On the basis of B.K. Nahru's lecture, the total amount of black money invested in general elections for both Parliamentary and State Assembly seats will be of the order of Rs. 1300 crores. The then Chief Election Commissioner, S.L. Shakdhar wrote in an article in 1980. "It is said that money comes from businessman, big and small, foreign countries and all sorts of questionable sources. It is not my purpose to fathom this. But there is a feeling that elections are tainted with money illegally obtained and this creates a doubt whether elections are indeed free, fair and pure."

Next come self employed professional people like doctors, lawyer consultants, chartered accountants etc. who have a tendency to conceal income with a view to avoiding tax liability. The Direct Taxation Enquiry Committee mentioned: "Black money and tax evasion which go hand in hand have also the effect of seriously undermining the equity concept of taxation and warping in progressiveness. Together they throw a greater burden on honest tax-payers and lead to economic inequality and concentration of wealth in the hand of the unscrupulous in the country." It is common knowledge, according to the Santhanam Committee, that some portion of the tax avoided or evaded is shared by many including the assessing officers.

Economic necessity has encouraged some who could not resist temptation. In India the attitude of the people is one of apathy and can be described as a bribe taken by a peon is called bakshish and a clerk, mamool. It is *rishwat* when accepted by a senior official. A Minister takes it in the name of "party funds". The bribe giver are also responsible to the aggravation of the problem. He may not expect anything done unlawfully. But, he wants rapid movement of files and quick decisions. Some members of the staff in an office have got into the habit of not doing anything till they are suitably rewarded. Some clever officials raise frivolous objections or quaries to deliberately delay matters. Ultimately public are harassed by such antisocial official in each and every sphere of life.

One of the major ill effects of black money in the country is that the prices of essential commodities like food-stuffs, fuel, clothing etc. go on increasing every year, given rise to inflation. This is caused by hoarding and black marketing of essential commodities by the businessmen who have enormous amount of black money. The main reason for the sorry state of affairs is that the politicians can hardly take effective steps against black marketeers and economic offenders who are their financiers at time of election.

Another impact of black money is the emergence of antisocial elements causing phenomenal increase in crimes like murder, bank robbery, dacoity and bridge burning. There is a widespread belief that criminals are patronised by people with black money.

The Prevention of Corruption Act, 1947 is a social legislation and was enacted to make more effective provision for the prevention of bribery and corruption. In spite of the various laws aimed at prevention of profiteering, undeserved income reach the hands of businessmen, professionals and serviceman in an innumerable forms. Although the system should be geared to allow only the due incomes as a main current of public opinion to different sections of people, yet secondary efforts have to be made to achieve the object by the system of direct taxation. Direct taxation have acquired special socio-economic significance and the main current has placed much reliance on them for the purpose of rationalising disparities in individual incomes and wealth. Sri N. Sanjiva Reddy after assuming the office of the President of India in 1978 stated that -"the generation of black money and its related offshoots such as corruption in elections, demoralisation of public services and deterioration of standards in public life should be curbed with a strong hand". The Choksi Committee set up by the Government of India on direct taxes has in October 1978, submitted a voluminous report covering both substantive and management problems. The Committee has recommended enactment of a single integrated code to cover the administrative and management of four main direct taxes -- Income tax, gift tax, property tax and surtax on company profits. But the decision of the Government under the Taxation Laws Act, 1978 to exempt political parties from wealth tax as well as from income tax, keeping aside the recommendations of the Choksi Committee is quite disappointing and showed a critical biasness. The Administrative Reform Commission has considered the question of corruption at the political level. It has suggested a permanent authority to keep a continuous vigilance over Ministers, by setting up a Lokpal on the same modal as the "Ombudsman" in the Scandinavian countries. A new Bill should provide that the action initiated on the recommendation of the Lokpal should be supervised by an authority independent of the Government. Sri Har Govind, in an article published in the Republic day issue of "*Mainstream*", 1979 suggested the following specific guidelines on the action against corrupt politicians:

(i) Legislators who are in employment of private undertakings should declare the facts. They should not approach the Ministers or officials in respect of such concerns.

(ii) Ministers should not collect party fund.

(iii) The system of wealth returns by legislators to their own party has not been effective. There is no statutory compulsion for compliance. Political expediency may deter the party to take action against defaulters or persons making false declarations. These returns should be scrutinised by an independent organisation, assisted by officers of proven integrity having experience of investigation of valuation problems.

(iv) An independent non-official organisation of merchants should be formed as vigilance chamber against corruption in the private sector. It should be able to investigate cases and even launch prosecution. Experienced officers from Government and reputed companies may be seconded to the vigilance chamber to deal with corruption cases in the private sectors.

Corruption is a deep rooted phenomena and its eradication is not easy. But it can certainly be minimised by removing public apathy. Creation of strong public opinion against corruption, educating the younger generation about the evils of corruption and virtues of honesty, proper and effective implementation of available laws against corruption destroying the influence of black money which is a major source of corruption.

11

Corruption at the Bureaucratic Desk

Bureaucratic corruption is as old as government office. We hear of it in Babylon and in Rome, in Classical India of the third century B.C. and in many other countries. In the modern era it appears all over the world and in all spheres of life. Corruption is perennial and ubiquitous to be found in any and all systems of government. The problem, therefore, is not to account for its presence, but rather for its existence and extent. Use of public power for private advantage is a serious offence and the public servants exercising such power in illegal acts are the society's No. 1 enemy, because of the injury to the public interest. In India the civil services personnel are exercising key powers of the public offices and as such detachment of the acts done by Ministries on the one end and subordinate officers on the other end is not possible. Under many circumstances of illegalities and corruption, nexus between civil servants and politicians or civil servants and their subordinates or businessmen appears to be present.

Study of several instances of corruption from time to time including the study conducted by the Santhanam Committee in independent India suggests that three circumstances impel officials to break faith with their employer and seek additional forbidden sources of income. These are the salaries paid, the opportunities presented for illegal use of office and policing to mean both detection and punishment. Obviously, corruption will be most prevalent when salaries are low, opportunities great and policing weak. It will be infrequent when the reverse applies, and salaries are generous, opportunities few and policing strong. But, in case of civil services personnel, it has never been alleged that salaries for this group were too low in the conventional sense of being insufficient to support a customary standard of living. It was rather that the opportunities with which they were presented suddenly proliferated. This first occurred during the World War II, when controls were imposed on the economy.

To control the malady in 1946, the Delhi Special Police Establishment (DSPE) was set up with the specific task of investigating and prosecuting corruption in the Central Government. In 1964 it was absorbed into a newly created Central Bureau of Investigation (CBI) as its investigative arm. This is the only body of police organisation remains in the Central government. All other police forces are State responsibilities. Despite best efforts given by the CBI, it has not been possible to discover an increasing number of corrupt officials for manifold reasons. Though corruption may have contained, it has not been reduced. For this there seems to be two reasons. First, opportunities continue to abound. To take only a few instances, licences and permits ere required for a great number of activities, contracts have to be pieced for defence and other supplies, the nationalised banks extend credit to cultivators, many of whom are illiterate and easily duped. These departments that deal most directly with the economy are also the most corrupt. The C.B.I. Report for 1980 gives detail of cases dealt with in the courts. Of 172 convictions fifty three (31 per cent) were officials from the Ministry of Finance (thirty six being from the public sector banks), twenty five (15 per cent) from the Railways, Twenty one (12 per cent) from the Ministry of Communications (mainly posts and telegraphs) and fourteen (eight per cent) from the Ministry of Defence.

The second reason is weak policing. Prevention of corruption in the administration is primarily the responsibility of the departmental heads. But in practice they tend to see the fight against corruption as the task of the specialised agencies. Political corruption is one of the main reasons of weak policing on corrupt activities of the officials. When corrupt, the Ministers are unable to demand honesty in their civil servants with any degree of conviction. Very often they serve as a model and an excuse for the corrupt official. It has recorded regretfully that political corruption in India is increasing and involves even the very highest levels of government. One cannot therefore expect any policing effort to come from that quarter.

Corruption is a socio-economic offence and also called white collar crime. The white collar criminal is an avaricious criminal person. It is his greed that is the cause of his crime. Prevention and control of corruption has been and continue to remain as a burning issue in India as appears from the failure of efforts to combat it. We have had innumerable Commissions of inquiry on corruption. The Railway Corruption Inquiry Committee under Acharya Kripalani (1953), The Vivian Bose Commission (1962), the Santhanam Committee on Prevention of Corruption (1964), the Wanchoo Committee Report on Black Money (1971). We have set up Special Police Establishment and Vigilance units in departments of administration at the centre and similar units set up in States. We have Union Public Service Commission and State Public Service Commissions to see that people are selected on merit and not to favour friends or relatives. We have else laws to combat corruption. Time to time amendment of such laws is also done to implement it more effectively. The Prevention of Corruption Act 1947 has been amended in 1988. But, none of them have succeeded even to the slightest degree in reducing the general prevalence of corruption, nepotism, black marketing, adulteration of food and drink, adulteration of drug etc. The reasons are manifold and multiferous. A courtry where administration itself is corrupted cannot expect a corruption free public life. All the ideals of socialism and collective wealth which seem to inspire our law makers are subverted by the misuse of the enormous power and patronage placed in the hands of ministers and officials. On the official front, the forms of corruption are similar to that on the political front. The two parties have to reciprocate in order to earn money by illegal means, earn the favour of newsman getting relatives and friends jobs they are actually not qualified for or promotion, import quotas that sell in the black at steep premium and so on. The objective of the official of course is different from the politicians. Under the auspices of this system the guardians of law commit crimes. They and the underworld of crime and anti-social elements have mutually advantageous relations hold up men and protection of racketeers and regular stipends from brothels, gambling dens, narcotic pedlars and smugglers.

One of the Santhanam solutions against corruption was to reduce discretionary powers of different categories of government servants. Discretionary power is highest at bureaucratic level. Corrupt officials at this level misuse their discretionary power for personal gain causing injustice and deprivation. Companies and businessmen should be obliged to keen detailed accounts of the expenditure in their expense account. Normally it is the duty of the Income Tax officers to scrutinise these accounts. But, whenever an

Income-Tax officer feels that amounts have been spent for entertaining high officials, or other purpose for which satisfactory explanation is not forthcoming, it should be his duty to refer the matter to the chief vigilance officer in the department concerned.

Great care should be exercised in selecting officers for appointment to high administrative posts. Only these whose integrity is above board should be appointed to these posts. During British regime, the Indian Civil Service (I.C.S.) officers were working as key administrators in the government system. Although the I.C.S. ceased to function as a service of the Secretary of State for India after the 15th August, 1947 when the Indian Independence Act, 1947 was enforced, its members were automatically appointed to corresponding posts under the Crown in connection with the affairs of the dominion of India or of a Province by virtue of the provisions of Sub-Clause (1) of Clause 7 of the Indian (Provisional Constitution) Order, 1947. Similar to the I.C.S., Indian Administrative Service (I.A.S.) were erected in the same pattern and conditions of service in the independent India and thereby the old bureaucratic framework retained. I.A.S. Officers are the key personalities forming the administrative machinery in the country. The State Civil Service officers along-with I.A.S. officers managing the administration in States. Several forms of corruption appear at different levels. A bribe taken by a peon is called "bakshis" and a clerk "mamooli". It is *rishwat* or *utkoch* when accepted by a senior official. A Minister takes it in the name of party funds. Some clever officials raise frivolous objections or queries to deliberately delay matters. The senior officers who are corrupt and incapable to deal with matters of concerned administration are accentric in nature and try either to victimise or suppress the junior officers who are not submissive to their corrupt activities. Administrative delays are one of the major causes of corruption. Quite often delay is deliberately contrived so as to obtain some kind of illicit gratification.

Under the prevailing system of administration, the number of bureaucrats has increased enormously with the result that decisions are avoided, responsibility shrinks and papers are floated up and down the hierarchical ladder, thus delaying decisions and keeping people waiting for unduly long periods. The bureaucracy must be made accountable not only for its actions but also its inaction in view of the current tendency that safety and profit lie in doing nothing. Among all the corrupt public servants, bureaucrats are most advantageous group by way of acting as disciplinary authority, A bias administrator may take his defence against corruption more advantageously than his subordinates. So, it is necessary to have an inspection agency that would carry out random checks at all levels of the administration to ensure quick disposal of cases and detect corruption and delay at all levels. Efficiency, honesty, merit and performance are to give more importance than to mere seniority for promotion at all levels specially at the higher echelons. Creation of laws against corruption as proved not at all effective to deal with corruption. Under the prevailing circumstances the custodian of laws are the law breakers.

12

Public Apathy Towards Corruption

Corruption typically connotes the abuse of public office for personal gain. Any employee, who corruptly accepts gift as an inducement for doing or refraining from doing anything in relation to his employer's business affairs, commits an offence, as does anyone who corruptly offers or provides such gifts. This concept of corruption was given in the Report of the Gaming Board for Great Britain, 1976. The problem of corruption is complex having roots and ramifications in society as a whole. Corruption is not a new offence in our country. It existed in India or elsewhere since ancient time. Kautilya in his *Arthasastra* refers to the various forms of corruption prevalent in his times. Corruption existed in other countries of the world also, similar to India. Paul H Dauglas, Senator from Illinois pointed out in his book on *'Ethics of Government* that corruption was rife in British public life till a hundred years ago and in USA till the beginning of this century. But it has observed that in spite of continuous efforts made to prevent corruption by societies since primitive time, generating public authority from the minimum in early days to the maximum in modern days, corruption has been increasing in a geometrical progression throughout the days.

Corruption is confined not only to a particular level of

officials or workers, but it also extends to all levels from top to bottom. The unconscious sanction of corruption at various levels is the outcome of some factors, of which the rise of the get-rich-quick politicians, and earning of money and wealth by dishonest employees of government, semi-government and private organisations are important. In our country, a bribe taken by a peon is called "bakshish" and by a clerk "mamooli". It is *rishwat* when accepted by a senior official. A Minister takes it in the name of "party funds". In a sense corruption is perennial and ubiquitous to be found in any and all systems of government. The problem, therefore, is not to account for its presence, but rather for its extent in a specific situation at a particular time.

Corruption in each and every walk of life has been in innumerable forms. Despite the appointment of several Commissions of inquiry and the preventive measures suggested by them over the past two decades and a half since the appointment of the Santhanam Committee on Prevention of Corruption, the problem in India has been growing unchecked and its dimensions increasing day by day. It starts from the top echelons and reaches the lowest level in the society, with the result that one cannot think of living honestly even if one aspires and yearns to do so. The real picture is that each individual's corruption is limited only by the limited scope he finds for it. From the public man to the common man it is the speedy wheel of corruption which motivates activity. But it is the common man who suffers the most, both in terms of evil effects of corruption and the iron hands of the law. According to Suresh Kohli, the critical analyst of the phenomenon of corruption, the law almost never touches the big man, the important public figure responsible for the destiny of the nation. Corruption in its dimensions spreads over the administration, politics, professions, Houses of God, press, arts, cinema, literature and so on.

The gravity of the crime is increasing day by day not only in India, but also in other parts of the world. Some countries could control corruption with their effective mechanism. It is very difficult to control corruption in the countries where administration itself is corrupted. Bureaucratic corruption in countries is as old as government office. We hear of it in Babylon and in Rome, in classical India of the third century BC, in the pre-reformation Catholic Church and in the Spanish empire, to come no closer to our own day. India has the longest history of anti-corruption work. The governments, past and present, both at the Centre as well as in States also assured to implement effective measures against corruption. However, the situation in India has not improved. In spite of having establishments like Vigilance Departments, Administrative Department and other agencies, the number of cases detected and of persons convicted are negligible in comparison to the actual figure. For this there seems to be two reasons. First, opportunities for corruption continue to abound. Secondly, there is the fall of integrity among politicians, administrators and other civil servants. As G S Bhargava stated in an article published in "*Mainstream*" in 1989, the fall of integrity among Ministers is common. In India's democratic polity, corruption had perennially been a live issue even before the advent of Rajiv Gandhi with his involvement in a series of scandals from Boeing to Bofors. Morarji Desai as the Deputy Prime Minister in the Indira Gandhi Government was accused of conniving at his son's dubious ways of getting rich by trading favours with business houses. Subsequently, as the Janata Prime Minister, Sri Desai was put in the dock by his number two in the Cabinet, Choudhury Charan Singh. The different Communist factions in Kerala charged one another with corruption and bribery. Abdul Rehman Antulay, an ex-Chief Minister of Maharashtra, was charged with gross misconduct of corrupt practices during his tenure as Chief Minister for the period from 1980 till he submitted his resignation on January 12,1982. Voices against corruption of Ministers and MLAs were raised in wide variations from State to State, through in lenient persuasion. Sri B.K. Nehru as seasoned Bureaucrat, said in a public lecture in 1980. It was estimated that the cost of an election in a Parliamentary Constituency was Rupees five lakhs to Rupees twenty lakhs against the ceiling on election expenses of Rupees one lakh, and that in a State Assembly constituency between Rupees one lakh and Rupees five lakhs against the ceiling of Rupees fifty thousand. The total cost to the parties and the candidates was colosal. The system has tended to generate into a more direct relationship between the money contributed and the favour granted. Once this nexus was accepted as a valid commitment of the democratic culture, not even the most powerful leader could stop the advance of corruption. The then Election Commissioner, S.L. Shakdhar wrote in an article in 1980, the corrupt politicians are very interested to sit in legislature in the pursuit of power only". Sri N Sanjiva Reddy, after assuming the office of the President of India in 1978, stated that "the generation of black money and its related offshoots such as corruption in elections, demoralisation of public services and deterioration of standard in public life should be curbed with strong hand. The Administrative Reform Commission has considered the question of corruption at the political level. It has suggested a permanent authority to keep a continuous vigilance over Ministers by setting up a Lokpal on the same model as the "Ombudsman in the Scandinavian countries. The Santhanam Committee found that the ultimate sources of corruption were:- (i) Ministers (ii)

Legislators (iii) Political parties and (iv) Industrialists and Merchants who seek favour from these three. But the Committee's recommendation regarding these ultimate sources of corruption have not received serious attention.

Creation of a social climate both among the public servants and the general public, in which bribery, illegal gratification and corruption in any other form may not flourish, will perhaps be a strong measure to fight corruption in public life. The law can only define a corrupt practice. The law-enforcer can only apprehend, and the law courts can only punish those brought before it. But the corrupt are too many and their accomplices too large in number.

The ingenuities of these Artful Dodgers are simply stupendous. Only a few of the corrupt are caught in the legal net. The society itself has to wage a war against its corrupt members. Public vigilance should be the basis of any anti-corruption strategy. It lies with the public which should be prepared to put up a stiff fight against corruption. For every corrupt officials, there are hundreds of members of the public wanting to make use of him. It will, therefore, be very difficult to tackle this growing evil unless we mobilize the best elements in society to fight it.

13

Police Force as Law Enforcement Machinery

In all the systems of government, now existed in different countries of the world the law represents the collective conscience of society. The Police force represents as principal law enforcing agent. So, the Police as law enforcement machinery ought to be the defender and keeper of that collective conscience. Exercise of police powers delegated by the statute is an essential state function which even a modern welfare state has to discharge in the governance of the country. The State exercises police functions through the agency of the Policeman, who enforces the law, maintains the public order, regulate the traffic, keep the lawless elements in check, brings the offenders to book and by his constant vigil preserve the coherence and solidarity of the social structure. The Police force is to protect the social order and not to work as a tool in the hands of the party in power as recorded in public mind. It has every right to disobey the illegal orders of the superiors for the interest of the welfare society. In order to mitigate the objectives of maintaining social order a Policeman must have the courage to disobey illegal orders even though it may emanate from the chief executive of the State. For this purpose the policeman is to depend on his honesty and sense of values.

The interplay between politics and police focusses

exclusively upon the external influences and controls that are illegal and improper. There are cumbersome examples within the country to show how the external influences that emanates from the federal state and local levels of government can illegally and unethically disrupt the mission, effectiveness and morale of a police department. So it is imperative that Police administrators understand and be able to cope with the dynamic external political forces operating within their communities. The extent to which they can do this will reflect significantly their ability to accomplish their law enforcement mission. Simultaneously the operation of the Police as with the operation of any other administrative agency that exercises governmental authority must be subject to effective legislation and judicial review and control. Accountability to police action conforms to the system of checks and balances.

Police as principal law enforcement agency of the State have the undoubted duty to bring predators to book without any fear or favour. Existence of effective government capable of maintaining law and order and of ensuring adequate social and economic conditions of life for the society depends on the efficacy of law enforcement by the police mission. To be able to induce others to obey the laws of society the Policeman must himself obey them first, with his example set before them, people will seek his help and protection and also to assist him in his noble task. He must be the leader amongst men. Leadership is the process of influencing organisational members to use their energies willingly and appropriately to facilitate the achievement of the Police department. By using their energies appropriately meant that morally and legally accepted means are employed in the discharge of duties. A Police personnel is to discharge some of basic duties such as—duty to uphold individual liberty, duty not to ignore the rights of the accused etc. the

Police leader is responsible for three equally important, but essentially different broad responsibilities:

1. Making work productive and subordinates achieving
2. Fulfilling the mission of the Police department, and
3. Producing impacts.

Human beings desire security and almost everywhere their lot in life is insecurity under the prevailing environment with anti-social activities. It is obvious that the consciousness of insecurity has become a global phenomenon. One needs no more than a cursory glance at newspapers, special reports or current affairs programmes on the media in India and elsewhere to become convinced that the attainment of personal security for ordinary men and women looms now larger as an aspiration than anything else. The problem of personal insecurity in society is often causes harmful effects in global phenomenon such as ever-deepening economic recession, the drying of markets, declining world trade, the growing gap between rich and poor and the resultant erosion of the living standards and even livelihood of individuals and families. Under such a circumstance the fruitful and honest discharge of statutory duties by Police Department at all levels becomes a dire necessity.

The code of conduct for the Indian Police says—"The Police are essentially a law enforcement agency. They should not question the propriety or the necessity of any duly enacted law. They should enforce the law firmly and impartially without for or favour, malice or vindictiveness and in that way a policeman becomes a living embodiment of the rule of law. Law does not permit perversion of its process for the purpose of feretting out crime either by fear or force or by other means equally objectionable. Despite difficulty the detective process must harmonise with fair and human standard."

It has however not to be admitted that there is another side of the picture which must also be taken into account. A country's legal system should not be such as would permit hundreds of wrongdoers to escape the law. Every unjust acquittal puts the innocent victim to the hazards of a new offence. Reforms in the legal system at least in certain provisions are needed to avoid mistrust of the law. For instance there is scope for unjust acquittal of criminal due to ban imposed on the use of police statement and confession made to the police by the Code of Criminal Procedure and the Indian Evidence Act, respectively. This mistrust of the law has a demoralising effect on the investigating police as a whole and quite a few of them feel in utter desperation.

With a view to minimising the problems of Police functioning as required to the extent in the changing society and with the scientific and technological advancement a response strategy is to be planned and implemented. On the street and in the communication centre, the dominant theme of the organisation and management of police operations is to respond as rapidly as possible to incoming calls for service. Scarcity of resources and instruments compels some delay. The main activity of police is petrol-involving cars roving on petrol not only for order maintenance and crime prevention purposes, but also to be in good position to respond rapidly. For disseminating effective service by the police force the police stations and other communication centres should be increasingly equipped with computer aids and other essential equipments.

14

Averting Criminal Holocaust: A Need of the Hour

Crime in the present day society have been increasing day by day in a wide dimension. It has always vied with economic and social matters as the gravest public concern. Unemployment and economic problems may raise anxieties about standard of living and well being, but crimes threatens life itself and potentially exposes everyone's person and property to risk from predators. The alarmed reaction of public to criminality may be regarded as a form of moral panic. News on incidence of crimes in various forms like murder, rape, abduction, kidnapping appears in daily news papers creating panic to public mind. Crimes disturbs the social and the moral order and affects some persons adversely. Statistics on crime show that crime is on the increase and this serious increase in appaling should not be allowed to continue in our society if we want the existence of our society.

In dealing with crime we may note that with the gaining ground of the theory of determinism and development radical school of penal reform, pathological and psychiatric remedies ere ranking in the forefront. Cut of two types of measures—re-educative and punishment against criminals, the former is beneficial in case of general criminals and the latter is appropriate in case of recidivists. Robberies, frauds, thefts, abduction, murder and kidnaps which are on the increase are mostly the result of the very grave extent of poverty, unemployment and political infections. An effective deal with the criminals is possible only through liquidation of the factors creating criminal behaviour of people particularly of youngsters. Want of employment and the growing and evergrowing population should be checked with perspective planning in a long term and short term basis. But the success of such planning depends upon the sincerity and honesty of the Central as well as State agencies. Punishment alone is no answer. The factors in the causation of crime are physical ailments and organic and functional mental ailments coupled with an environment favourable for antisocial outbursts. A criminal act may be the result of neurosis or psychosis or of susceptibility to crime by reason of mental defect coupled with some environmental factors or some emotional disability. It is really the mind that controls actions, if the mind is derranged, defective or feeble we must take appropriate measurer, for a cure by removing the defect or to the fortification of the faculty.

Some other causes of crime prevalent in our society are—maladjustment or lack of organisation of the traits of personality, suggestibility, imitation, the unwholesome influence of bad company or undesirable environment, lack of reverence and religion, lack of moral culture, alcoholism, addiction to drugs, lack of education and training, mental conflicts, society's apathy and lethargy in its relationship with criminals, neglect and delay in checking juvenile delinquency, faulty theories of punishment, lack of home training of a proper type, broken homes, disgusting home environment, too much of interference by parents or too slack a discipline, trouble caused by step parents, drunkenness at home and avarice.

Avarice and mental conflict are the two most common causes of crimes of the present day society. Avarice leads not only to crime by individuals, but also to what are known as "war crimes" by nations. The spirit of aggrandisement lead a nation prepared for war to pounce upon other nations or to keep other nations under unfair subjectivity. A militarist tradition and a world broken up into a number of independent sovereign States, which are greatly greedy for power and domination have brought about the present distress. It is clear from the prevalent circumstances of the past and present that selfishness and avarice have been the cause of men's decline from spiritual eminence to barbarous degradation and miserable decline.

Mental conflict is the most important factor in the causation of the present day crime. Mental conflict may arise in a number of ways. It may arise due to existence or prevalence of unjust law and unjust activities. In such cases conflict of ideals is the result of moral excellence, soul's loftiness and divinity.

Another kind of mental conflict may arise out of an evil desire to gain by unfair means. So many murders are actuated by the desire to get material gain over, or robbery of the victim's property. Under such type of mental conflict crime is said to be caused by" a willful response to the temptations of the devil", the type of crime caused by man's choice of evil or caused by his inability or feeblemindedness to select the right path.

Removal of the cause of the crime concerned and preventing recurrence are of great importance. A good prevention is ensured by the method of education—the re-organisation of the disorganised personality or the removal of the maladjustment, by persuation suggestion and re-education. Removal of the conflict of mind causing crime is a very difficult task. All types of conflicts cannot be removed easily. Inadequate and improper measures may cause more harm rather than curing. So, such programmes should be as per norms and principles of criminology. That conflict which is caused by inadequacy of training in group ideals, by the lack of moulding, reshaping, developing, modifying and culturing the temperamental traits, and the innate propensities can only be removed and prevented by re-adjustment in conformity with healthy moral principles, habits and right ways of thinking. A person not adequately cultured in the sentiments and not adequately trained in the social ideals is likely to disregard the law of his land.

Prevention can be brought about by personality adjustment through education, public welfare, public health and judicial administration. The environmental factors also must be taken into account. Defective traits of personality are often potent factors in criminality. Personality is the net sum of those traits and sentiments which constitute human nature. The development, modification, moulding and reshaping of these traits, giving them a new social birth, depend upon education, experience, group life and environmental factors.

Lack of value education in the real sense is a potent cause of moral depravity. It is essential then to turn to the question of shaping of character. It is through the moulding of propensities and potentialities, the formation of good habits, that a good character can be shaped. Ideal education involves such harmonious and integrated development of the mind and its mutual tendencies as would make it capable of facing any crisis, and as would enable its recipient to think, say and act rightly and harmoniously.

A misdirected propensity may cause the culmination of conduct in the commission of a crime. The remedy lies therefore in the reconditioning of the propensities so that the same may lead to harmlessness of purpose, nobleness of goal and beneficence of action and the individual concerned then fails not in his mode of thinking and falls not into the fell of unsocial conduct.

Considering all the relevant points of criminological principles and norms the present and prospective Government both at the centre and in States may prepare perspective plans for eradicating crimes from our society in a phased manner.

15

Reservation: A Debatable Issue

When at time a major section of population in India become frustrated on reservation issue still existed as Constitutional mandate even after crossing half century of independence which had to be discontinued after ten years of its implementation, the policy of reservation in promotion quota for SCs and STs offering opportunity to the same candidate to avail this facility repeatedly at the cost of total deprivation to mertorious shiftable and senior employees belonging to communities other than backward castes, further aggravated the situation.

During the last decade, hardly a year passed without any violence by anti-reservationists in one or a few other states. During V P Singh regime the violence spread over the Centre in a serious turn after acceptance of the Mandal Commission recommendations. The violence against reservation provisions appeared intermittently in different states and in the Centre indicates that a general climate of acceptance of reservation policies has been lacking. The policy of reservation in promotion quota has further added to the accumulation protest which is growing potent with mounting unemployment and ignorance of merit and suitability of candidates belonging to castes other than SCs and STs. It is necessary at this moment to re-examine the policy to have a positive correlation between traditional;

social, and educational backwardness and economic status regarding the castes other than the traditionally backward castes. Under no circumstances the policy of reservation in promotional posts can be justified for benefitting the same candidate repeatedly with the facilities of reservation. This benefit should be available only once in service.

The Supreme Court has passed an order that where there is direct recruitment to a service, equality of opportunity would require that the posts be advertised. However, it is well known that after initial recruitment, appointment to higher posts in the service are at times made partly promotion and partly directly, or at times wholly by promotion. When the appointment is partly by promotion and partly by direct recruitment, it would be necessary to advertise the posts. Where however, the appointment is by promotion among those already employed, equality of opportunity does not necessarily require that the appointment should be advertised, but it does require that the case of each person eligible for promotion should be fairly considered. In Paramatma Sharan-V-Chief Justice (A Raj 13. 1964), it was held with reference to the post of Assistant Registrar and Secretary to the Chief Justice that the equality of opportunity contemplated by Art, 16 did not mean that in every case of appointment or recruitment in service or promotion, the State should invite applications for such appointment or promotion, "... the emphasis is that as between A and B there should be no discrimination in the matter of appointment. The question of the nature and extent of the reservation which can be made in public employment has been considered by the Supreme Court in several cases, in Venkataraman-V-Madras (A.S.C. 229. 1951), a communal G.O. of the Madras government which reserved posts not only for Harijans and backward classes, but also for other communities, namely, Muslims, Christians, non-Brahmins (Hindus) and

Brahmins was held to violate Art. 16. The scope of Art 16[4) was considered in Devadasan-V-Union (4 S.C.R. 680. A.S.C. 179.1964) under the following circumstances, by a Government of India Resolution dated September 13, 1950 as modified by supplementary instructions dated January 28, 1952 and Office Memorandum dated May 7, 1955, the government reserved a certain percentage of vacancies for SCs and STs. adopting the principle of "carry forward" in the second and third year. The actual effect of the carry forward rule for the year in question was that a little over 64 per cent of vacancies were reserved for SCs and STs. By a majority of 4 to 1 the Supreme Court held that Art. 16 conferred a right on each individual citizen seeking employment or appointment to an office under the State and that in order to effectuate that right, each year of recruitment must be considered by itself, and the reservation for backward communities each year should not be so excessive as to create a monopoly or to interfere unduly with the legitimate claims of other communities.

Art 16(4) was proviso or an explanation to Art 16(1) and the opening words of Art. 16[4) nothing in this Article shall prevent etc... could not be so construed as to nullify the express guarantees contained in Art. 16(2). A proviso or an exception cannot be so interpreted as to nullify or destroy the main provision. To hold that unlimited reservation of appointments could be made under clause [4) would in effect efface the guarantee contained in clause (1) or at best make it illusory. An esprit de corps is an essential element for an efficient and harmonious public service. It is not possible to maintain an esprit de corps' for any appreciable period of time, if the pride in the service is destroyed, first by division in the services based on caste, and even more, where reservation are made in promotion posts in favour of members of SCs and STs who are not rationally comparable in merit to the persons left out. It is not legal and at the same time not possible to brush aside facts and opinions recorded in Supreme Court decisions on reservation issue as vote catching or vote losing issue. Justice Krishna Iyer was aware of this when he said to politicise this provision for communal support is to subvert the solemn undertaking of Art 16 (A). In this situation the role of a federal court as the interpreter and guardian of the Constitution comes into play, and the exercise by the court of its power would be welcomed by most politicians as taking a load of their backs.

In C.A. Rajendran—V- Union (1 S.C.R. 721. A.SC. 507. 1968) when the Railway Board found that quota reservation were harmful from the point of view of the efficiency of Railway service, the reservations were withdrawn, the challenge to be withdrawn failed. Again there is an instructive passage in A Periakaruppan-V-TN (2 S.C.R, 430. A.SC. 2303. 1971) and although it refers to reservations under Art. 15(4), the same principles apply to reservations, under Art 16(4). Hegde said ... all the same the government should not proceed on the basis that once a class is considered as a backward class, it should continue to be backward class for all times. Such an approach would defeat the very purpose of the reservation because once a class reaches a stage of progress which some modern writers call as take, off stage then competition is necessary for their future progress. The Government should always keep under review the question of reservation of seats and only the classes which are really socially and educationally backward should be allowed to have the benefit of reservation.

Reservation of seats should not be allowed to become a vested interest. The fact that candidates of backward classes have secured about 50 per cent of the seats in the general pool does show that the time has come for a de novo' comprehensive examination of the question. It must be remembered that the government's decision in this regard is open to judicial review."

A person who but for the reservation, would have walked into the higher post on his merit must be more than human, if he is not deeply resentful of the injustice done to him and of his having to serve under a person vastly his inferior in merit. Art. 16[4) of the Constitution does not confer any-fundamental right on backward classes as regards reservation of posts whether it be at the stage of ' recruitment or promotion. It is only an enabling provision which conferred a discretionary power, on the state to make a reservation of appointment in favour of backward class of citizens which in its opinion not adequately represented in the service of State.

In making reservations for appointments or posts, the government has to take into account not only the claims of the members of the backward classes, but also the maintenance of efficiency of administration which is of paramount importance. The State government is fully responsible to give justice to all communities within the constitutional boundaries in the way of reservation or unreservation. The proposition laid down in C.A. Rajendran -vs-Union of India and others (A.I.R. 1968. SC 507) is that it is discretionary with the government to provide for reservation. Even if by an order earlier the government adopted a policy of reservation, it could give it up by a subsequent order.

My view on the issue on the basis of above contentions is that reservation in appointment for backward classes may be justified under the prevailing situation for an earmarked extension period but it should be provided once in service only. Reservation in promotional posts is excessive and injustice.

16

Quota Policy Needs Re-examination

The agitations on the issue of reservation in Government jobs and seats in educational institutions by those for and against it has made it clear that a re-examination of the relevant policy is necessary. The idea behind introducing reservations in the Indian Constitution for the Scheduled Castes and Scheduled Tribes, whether in education or in jobs was to help them to come up to become strong enough to join the other sections of the community on terms of equality. It was acknowledged that they would need special concessions for a short period before they could hold their own in open competition for jobs as well as education. Accordingly the reservation provisions were made in the Indian Constitution under Art. 16(4) and 16(4) originally for a period of ten years only. Reservations were a temporary measure and were to be removed as soon us possible to meet the objective of creating a casteless society which was the aim of the founding fathers of the Constitution. But instead of abolishing it, the Government has so far taken a policy of extending its terms repeatedly for ten/years. In each time of its expiry making no hope of abolishing it in near future. Already there is a significant amount of resentment about reservations as indicated by agitations in States from time to time. There is also a growing feeling that the same families, generation to generation come up to claim reservation benefits. Because a caste or tribe is indicated by birth and cannot be changed which is a major demerit of the reservation made on the basis of caste. Under reservation provisions implemented in different States as well as in the centre even an economically and socially advanced family may get the benefits of reservation by birth.

The process of economic development and the advance of civilisation have visibly weakened the caste traditions. The modern trend is towards liberalism, mutual accommodation and adjustment, recognition of merit as far as possible and not of birth as the determinant of one's occupation and status in society. Reservation in jobs and seats in educational institutions for SC and ST as per constitutional provisions was to uplift these backward castes to the level of others. But, as a matter of fact reservation as a means of bringing the deprived groups into the mainstream of national life seems to have been signal failure. The argument that, do reservation really help the majority from the backward classes and most handicapped among these ? How can a person from the backward classes coming from a village or an urban, slum reach the minimum level of educational requirement? The state of primary schools in rural areas or even in large parts of urban areas is deplorable enough. More than half the schools have no building. The reservation provisions alone without improvement of the basic facilities cannot help the backward classes to reach the objectives of Art. 15(4) and 10(4) of the Constitution. Although reservations are to help to improve the economic status, the other signs of backwardness, particularly the social stigma nevertheless remains intact. This is because the necessary collateral activities particularly that of building a social consciousness alongwith the policy of reservation was never done. At the same time a fresh wave of antagonism is created. It is also necessary to note that unlike in the case of SC and ST whose social and economic backwardness needs no proof, it is not so clear that there is a positive correlation between traditional, social and educational backwardness and economic status regarding others. There are undoubtedly other castes groups which continue to be both socially and educationally backward and economically poor even certain proportions of advanced castes. As such giving benefit on the basis of caste is to create a permanent weaker section and divide the society permanently.

There is a consistent charge in the recent years that politicians have used the reservation policy for their short term and partisan ends. Since its renewal in 1980 the discontent is gradually becoming more apparent. In 1980 there were some dissenting voices, but it was decided not to express this in public. To some it was abject surrender for a few votes and to some it was understanding of social problem. The underlining resentment became evident when the Mandal Commission presented the report to the government on 31-12-81. The Commission's report was tabled before Parliament in August, 1982, without any comment from the Government. From then onward opposition was asking for its implementation, but the prevailing Congress(I) Government did not take a decision in this regard. There are grave reservations about the recommendations among the intelligent, particularly because it brings caste as the main factor in the new scheme of things.

Mandal said in its report that 52.4 per cent of the people in the country belonged to the backward castes and the forward castes had to pay the price for suppression of backwards by their forefathers, He said that the benefits given to the SC and ST must be extended to Backward Castes and reservation of seats in the Government jobs and academic, institutions must be made for them. As a fraction over 22 per cent has already been reserved for the SC and ST and as the Supreme Court does not allow more than 50 per cent reservations. The Mandal Commission recommended 27 per cent reservations for the backward classes. This was so unacceptable that neither the Government nor the opposition parties to discuss the report in Parliament though occasionally some members raised the question. A constant criticism against the Mandal Commission's report was going on that it has placed caste at the centre of social and economic life, and not the individual and therefore it is contrary to the principle of individual freedom and to the spirit of the constitution. The Commission has justified its approach on the ground that equality between the unequals is to perpetuate inequality. At the same time it also says that what one calls talent is an amalgam of native environments and environmental privileges. Further it says, "Equality of opportunity is also a social principle because it ignores the many invisible and cumulative hindrances in the way of the disadvantaged, unless the children of the poor are taken from their parents at birth and brought up in middle-class homes, most are condemned to inequality of opportunity. And therefore it advocates the equality of results. During pendency of a decision on Mandal Commission's report other Backward Class Commissions were constituted by some of the State Government and recommended many provisions for their Slate. The Rama Commission appointed by the Gujarat Government suggested economic criterion to be the basis for deciding backwardness. While trying to implement the Rama Commission's report by Solanki Government, as election manifesto serious situation has been created in Gujarat and ultimately the Solanki Government had to be ousted from power. The demand of the anti-reservationists in

Gujarat was for scrapping of the entire reservation provisions.

Those who have been clamouring for the implementation of the Mandal Commission report would perhaps report that Mandal Commission's assignment being to review the reservation provisions no fresh review is necessary.

17

Educational Policy in Context of Development

The aim of education is to develop the reasoning and intellectual faculty of man and to develop a scientific temper in him. It aims at improving and advancing one's sensitivity, humanity and the aesthetic sense so that one may become a better human being. The development or our country was hindered during foreign rule and after foreign rule the country faced the difficult task of transformation of our society. Transformation of a society from the backward to an advanced state needs removal of illiteracy, superstition, irrationality and bigotry. In our successive educational policies, lot of experiments were conducted on., students by successive governments. Much has been done so far by the Government to remove illiteracy in the society by introducing educational policies relevant to both urban and rural environment. The policy to provide compulsory elementary education to every child should be strictly followed and all resources should be mobilised towards this objective. Development of a society needs its modernisation. On the contrary, modernisation is directly linked with literacy. So, unless the maximum number of people become literate, innovation of new ideas in the society is resisted. An educational policy, therefore, must ' aim at this objective of attaining literacy by masses in the society. The new thrust in elementary education given in the National Policy on Education, 1986, emphasising universal elementary education and universal retention of children upto 14 years of age is just and appropriate to our society.

Development of a society is directly linked with its existing culture, 'customs and social status along with literacy. A programme of literacy drive cannot attain success without social reform. Superstition of people' is one of the most important factors responsible for offering resistance to change through innovation of new ideas and techniques of development. Mankind is naturally not just a homogeneous mass, totally devoid of all Inner distinctions. Societal activities under a given, environment are aimed at using its forces, processes and substances and energy of highly varied natural resources. To fulfil this objective, human element as members of a society must accordingly be dynamic and innovation of culture. Historical records of the pattern of behaviour of human being suggests some measures, psychological, social, economical and educative to be taken for motivation of people towards acceptance of relevant cultures. Under certain circumstances, superstitious activities harmful to society must be prevented through introduction of code of law.

Development of people in a society does not mean in one direction. It means a total development that is social, economic, cultural, scientific and technological. All types of development are interconnected. It is not education of any kind that can take the country forward from poverty to prosperity. The educational system must be geared to help all types of development. The educational system which was set up in British days primarily at getting an adequate supply of candidate from middle class families with knowledge of English, and education in those days was too expensive. But it is surprising that even in post-independence years most parents look upon education as a means to get their children a job, preferably a desk job either as a big shot or as a clerk. But our problem of poverty and under development cannot be solved by unproductive employment. It is their productivity that must be improved by the right kind of education. It was felt by our planners, educationists and governments both at the Centre and in States in the independent India that a bold new orientation to our educational system was necessary, and accordingly, efforts have so far been made to find out a relevant educational policy in our country. Right from Mudaliar Commission on Education, 1952, to the National Education Policy, 1980, a series of recommendations on the educational system have been made. Ultimately, the National Education Policy, 1986 has been implemented with ambitious objectives. But during, the past few years of introduction of the National Education Policy, some experiences in both positive and negative sides have been acquired. On the one hand, we have a growing abundance of highly qualified people, which enable us to claim that we have the world's third largest reservoir of scientific and technical personnel, while on the other hand, we have to confess to having the world's largest number of illiterates.

Prior to introduction of the New education policy in 1986, there was the old one of 1968 in which the very first clause stated that the objective of education is 'to promote national progress, a sense of common citizenship and culture and strengthen national integration'. Now there is a stress on quality. But, it is very much difficult to achieve a value system in a caste-structured society like ours. It is also unfortunate that the caste-oriented cultures, instead of being reduced after Independence, have further entrenched and fortified, regardless of Indian Constitution. The question is, how a New Education Policy is going to change that.

During Mao's regime, the Chinese were able to introduce drastic changes in their educational system. Some were disastrous; but at least they were able to use the civic discipline enforced by the Cultural Revolution to create equality and a sense of citizenship in their schools. With a view to mobilising the resources and achieving a desired goal in our country, a relevant system of education should to be introduced, removing the existing lacuna of the educational policy.

Ahead of us lie difficult, but hopeful years. These years will confront us tin with hard problems and hard choices. We will find the problem easier to solve and the choices easier to make if we constantly remind ourselves that our concern with educational policy is to produce capable and honest persons.

18

Drug Adulteration and Law

The health of the citizens ought to be the primary concern of any State. In order to secure better health to its citizens it falls upon the State to ensure that there is no adulteration in foodstuffs, drugs and cosmetics. The success of any health scheme of the State would depend not merely on the availability and supply of standard quality drugs but also on purity of foodstuff and cosmetics. To achieve this objective the State very often resort to prescription of standards of purity and quality of drugs and cosmetics. The Government both at the centre as well as in States lay rules and regulations to control the production, manufacture, distribution, sale etc. of drugs and cosmetics. The Drugs and Cosmetics Act, 1940 regulates the import into, manufacture, distribution and sale of drugs and cosmetics in the country. But, the breaching of the rules and regulations are on increasing day by day and adulteration of drugs and cosmetics is rampant these days. Similarly it is established fact that markets are filled by spurious drugs and harmful cosmetics. The problem of adulteration of drugs and also of production of spurious and substandard drugs are now-a-days posing serious threat to the health of the community. Considering the necessity to increase the penal actions to be more stringent against the antisocial elements indulging in the manufacture or sale of adulterated or spurious drugs or drugs not of standard quality which are likely to cause death or grievous hurt to the user amendment of the Act. has been made from time to time. The Amending Act. 68 "of 1982 provides penalties on a more rational basis as follows.

(a) The proposed scale of punishment in respect of the first offence shall be--

  (i) imprisonment for not less than five years which may extend to life and with fine of not less than rupees ten thousand for the manufacture, sale of adulterated or spurious drugs or drugs not of standard quality which are likely to cause death or harm,

  (ii) imprisonment for not less than one year which may extend to three years and fine of not less than rupees five thousand for manufacture and sale of any adulterated drug or manufacture and sale of drugs without a valid license,

  (iii) imprisonment for three years which may extend to five years and with fine of not less than rupees five thousand for manufacture or sale of spurious drugs,

  (iv) imprisonment for other offences shall be not less than one year, which may extend to two years and with fine.

(b) The proposed scale of punishment for subsequent offences shall be--

  (i) imprisonment for not less than two years which may extend to six years and with fine of not less than rupees ten thousand for manufacture or sale of adulterated drugs or manufacture and sale of drugs without a valid license,

  (ii) imprisonment for not less than six years which

may extend to ten years and with fine of not less rupees ten thousand for manufacture and sale of spurious drug,

(iii) imprisonment for a term for not less than two years which may extend to four years and with fine of not less than rupees one thousand or with both for other offences.

The main object of enhancing the degree of punishment under the Act is to prevent sub-standards in drugs presumably for maintaining high standards medical treatment. That will certainly be defeated if the necessary concomitants of medical or surgical treatment are allowed to he diluted; the very same evil which the Act intends to eradicate will also continue to subsist. Adulteration makes articles not merely unfit for human consumption but sometimes positively injurious and harmful to the consumers. Therefore it is often described as subtle murders practiced on the community. It mostly starts with the if manufacturers and then travels to the wholesalers and retailers. Adulteration is also committed by the retail salers.

Measures Prescribed

In spite of stringent measures prescribed in the Act, manufacture and sale of adulterated spurious or substandard drugs are increasing in a rampant way due to lack of affective implementation of the Act. Ample power are given by the Act. to enforcement authorities like Public Health officials right from Inspectors to the Director, Police Department and Civil administration for an affective implementation of the Act. Eventhough the total failure to prevent manufacture and sale of adulterated, spurious and sub-standard drugs in the market is becoming a serious concern of the masses. There are many causes of this total failure such as material defects in institution of cases against antisocial elements, lacuna in the Act for conviction under certain circumstances, negligence or corruption of enforcement authorities, lack of public consciousness to make public resentments of those antisocial activities, under-utilisation of analytical laboratories for prompt detection and penal action of the delinquents etc. In SK Amir-V-State of Maharashtra (1974), the facts were that the drug viz 95,000 capsules of seco Barbital Sodium which is a sedative agent, was found in a parcel which was in accused's possession when he was apprehended at the gate of railway station. The Supreme Court opined that the large quantity of 95,000 capsules in the possession of the accused left no room for doubt that he had stocked or kept the drug for sale. To prove an offence under Section 18 of the Drugs Act the prosecution must prove that the goods were stocked or exhibited for sale and not merely that they were stocked. This can be proved by direct or circumstantial evidence. In Ambulul D. Bhatt-V-State of Gujarat (1972) the accused was charged under Section 304--A, I.P.C. for rashly and negligently manufacturing a solution of glucose in normal saline which contained more than the permitted quantity of lead nitrate and some persons died on account of this solution having been administered, it was held that the mere fact that an accused contravenes certain rules or regulations in the doing of an Act which causes death of another does not establish untill the death was the result of a rash or negligent act or that any such act was the proximate and effective cause of the death. The Act causing the death "must be the cause causans; it, is not enough that it may have been the causa sine qua non".

The World Health Organisation has so far reported withdrawal of 37 drugs by certain countries due to adulteration or substandard quality out of which only 19 were not approved for marketing in India. It appears from this figure that sonic drugs which are not fit, for human consumption are still not banned in Indian market. For an effective control of drug menaces in India, a strong and effective infrastructural base for drug testing in addition to active and honest participation of both public and enforcement authorities is required.

19

Psychiatric Diseases as Crime Causation

The concept of disease in the psychiatric sciences cannot be defined or definitively established. In recent years however, etiological and social factors have been stressed in preference to symptomology. The tern mental abnormalities should be used when the condition is associated with particulars organic processes. It is hence maintained that a mental diseases *is* only present when its cause is pathological changes of the brain, there are several important differences between a disease and the so called abnormal conditions or states. Such mental states are permanent, consistent deviations from mental normality. Although the basis of the abnormality cannot be changed, tills does not mean that treatment will have no effect in mitigating some of its social consequences.

Treatment of mental diseases is very much important from the point of view of social and individual security as such diseases are important cause of crimes. There are two main groups of mental diseases viz., organic mental diseases and functional mental diseases. Organic mental diseases are those in which definite brain pathology is present. In functional mental or emotional no such pathology has yet been demonstrated, though even bio-chemical disorders are suspected to be present. In organic mental diseases there is often a permanent irreversible loss of intellectual efficiency known as dementia. Functional mental diseases are of two types the neuroses Crinor mental diseases and the psychoses. The neurotic illnesses comprise largely of patients with hysterical conversion or dissociation type of disorder, obsessive compulsive states and anxiety states. In case of dementia there may be loss of self-criticism and lack of capacity for fin discriminations especially in delicate moral issues, which may easily lead to crimes against decency. Later a mental condition arises causing difficulty in learning and conversation memory and orientation in time, place and person. Emotions becomes labile and moral sense is lost. Persons affected by this type of mental disease may commit crimes easily, especially of a sexual nature, as the patient is unaware of the repugnancy of his act. The causes of dementia may be senility, cerebrovascular disorders, hypertensive encaphalopathy due to extremely high blood pressure, inflamatory diseases of the brain like siphilis and encaphalitis of various types, head injury, brain tumour, and degenerative diseases. Excessive drinking habit and vitamin B_{-12} deficiency contribute to the formation of degenerative diseases. As a curative measure, vitamin or protein deficiency should be got over by proper food supply rich in vitamins and proteins. Society and the family should turn to be more attentive to the child and his physical and mental will being.

Patients of functional mental diseases that is neurosis and psychosis, are not usually commit serious typed of crimes, like murder for the patient can resist his impulse to commit such an act. Neuroses are generally considered to be diseases which do not have relevant, observable anatomical changes. Most psychiatrists presume that neuroses occur as a result of inadequate adjustment in either a momentary or a long lasting conflict situation,

Apart from the Kleptomanias (Pathological Steeling) of compulsive neurotic origin, neuroses are of criminological interest for two reasons. First increases anxiety sometimes leads to a crisis point in which there may be a risk of dangerous criminal acts such as rape, assault or homicide. Most often, such persons have no previous convictions. During socialisation, a connection is established between breaking a prohibition guilt feelings and punishment, where the psychological function of the punishment is to eliminate or at least reduce the feeling of guilt, in moat neurotic symptoms which contain a symbolic breaking of a prohibition, a somewhat unpleasant element of punishment is built in. This is the price that must be paid for the symbolic satisfaction of the urge. In the treatment of neuroses, psychotherapy, minor tranquillizers like meprobamate, chlorodizepepoxide, diazepam, should be utilized.

There are several type of psychoses such as schizophrenia, manic-depressive psychosis, Epilepsy, alcoholic psychosis, sonile psychsis, psychogenic psychoses. All these psychoses have several common symptoms, on inability to interact socially (Cautism); profounding change in emotional tone (Apathy), often a paradoxical character, and an apparent incoherence of the intellectual processes. For serious acute psychoses the condition will usually be so marked that the person will be hospitalised before he has time to commit any offence. And most of those who remain in the community, because their paranoid ideas do not attract attention, seldom translate these ideas into serious criminal acts. The manic phase is marked by euphoric mood producing increased self confidence, raving fantasies, optimism and restless activity. The melancholic or depressive phase shows the converse picture. The patient suffers from hypochrondia, an indefinite melancholy, decreased self confidence and a pessimistic attitude to life and is restrained in though and movement. Anxiety feelings and delusions, especially morbid guilt feelings and persecution mania are connected within this phase. In a high spirited mood creating mania with a lack of self control, the risk of committing libels, offences against public order, aggressive acts etc. are increased. Suicide is the greatest danger in the melancholic state. The drug "lithium" is useful in preventing attacks of mania.

Epilepsy may be the background of many typed of crimes. It arises from the temporal lobe of the brain, usually of the dominant cerebral hemisphere. The crime that results has an absence of premeditation or of motive and an absence of precaution, crimes committed may be extremely brutal, the patient following his crime to a revolting extreme. The epileptic should be psychologically managed to lead as normal a life as possible. Many drugs such as phenobarbitone, phenytoin-sodium and zarontin helps treatment of epilepsy. Alcoholic psychosis arises from alcohol poisoning. Acute alcohol psychosis do not create much problems in criminality as they usually lend to immediate hospitalisation. In legal psychiatry the lack of conscious control over the causes of the action is stressed. Senile psychoses such as senile demantia. Syphilitic Insanity, chronic encephalitis may cause derious crimes. For the treatment of such types of psychoses, use of drugs such as phenothiazines, reserpine, derivatives and gams-amino-butyric acid derivatives are particularly effective.

The main causal factors of psychogenic psychoses are family conflicts, sexual conflicts, death of near ones, catestrophic events, social crisis or imprisonment. Psychgenic psychoses are caused mostly by shock or sudden aggravation of a conflict which may have existed for some time. The characteristic symptoms are emotional states such as depression, exaltation, emotional paralysis, temper tantrums, disturbances of consciousness or paranoid syndromes. Depression of all sorts is very specifically treated by electro convulsive therapy. Anti-deptylene, diazepam and the stimulants are such drugs and are alone effective in many cases.

Another disease, "Oligophrenia" or mental deficiency" ranges from most severe cases of defects in intelligence, that is feeble mindedness or sub-normality to minor defects, so called dullness. Four stages of oligophrenia may be distinguished, debility, imbecility and idiocy. Mental age is determined by ability of the subject to solve a series of questions or problems. These are graded so as to reflect the previously determined abilities of groups of normal children of various ages. The tests include many different kinds of problems as it is considered desirable to avoid testing a limited number of special abilities or only to measure the presence of school Knowledge. Those who are more seriously deficient will usually be under care and generally present no social risk. If they have the opportunity to commit crimes, these will be the result of instinctive drives or excitement. Such crimes are often of sexual in nature. The less several imbeciles are usually not dangerous as a sole result of their intelligence defect. This defect can often be compensated socially through the will power and emotional feelings of the person concerned. However a special crime risk occurs, when low intelligence is coupled with character defects preventing the processes of compensation.

Dullness manifest itself during childhood in difficulties in carrying out school work. They are also inferior in purely mental skills and rate of work. It is obvious that the dull are exposed to a special risk of crime, partly as a result of their reduced ability to foresee and consider the consequences of their acts and partly as a result of having low social status and consequently, reduced opportunities of achieving an income comparable to that of their companions. The latter may lead to character defects and disharmonious personality development, which in itself, way influence the crime risk. If our society is not conscious about the gravity of the danger from the feeble minded and not place them under care of one part or another, it may be expected that more of them would become criminal. Other social institutions such as school system, labour exchanges especially those for the handicapped, unemployment insurance and social aid also play a preventative role.

A most serious type of mental disease known as psychopathy has become particularly widespread since the 1920s. In a report of the Danish Psychopathy Commission, published in 1931, the following types of psychopathy are described (1) impassionate (2) excited (3) emotionally unstable (4) reserved (5) emotionally cold or callous and (6) morally deficient. The antisocial and asocial tendencies corrected with various forms of psychopathy are of great criminological interest. Psychopathic patients tend to commit various types of serious crimes such as libel, fraud and vagrancy, political crimes, unscrupulous murder and robbery, terrorism and property offences. It is known that pathological character development can arise as a consequence of traumatic brain damage, or harmful perinatal experience. These people are 'anti-social' personalities incapable of forming loyalties to others or to any groups or codes of living. They are jealous and callous and have no sense of responsibility. In spite of punishment they do not charge their anti-social behaviour. They lack social sense or judgement. They lack a socialized supremo and have no ideals. They are prone to serve outbursts of temper in which assault or even murder may occur. In recent years there has been a trend away from the consideration of psychopathy as incurable, towards attempting the adjustment of psychopaths to the demands of society.

This is particularly important in the case of the criminal psychopathy. Diagnosis of psychopathy, in order to be useful in treatment, must be made by a psychiatrist working without knowledge of the person's criminality.

The value of psychiatry in the prevention of crime by the curing of mental ailments and by providing of proper treatment for individual offenders cannot be overemphasised. Psychiatry can help our Law courts in deciding on questions of responsibility.

20

Combating Terrorism: Reflections on Law, Order and Politics

Terrorism is a worldwide phenomenon which has unfortunately now come to stay in India and elsewhere polluting to all the States, regions, sub-regions and so on. Terrorist is the person who creates an overwhelming impulse of fear or horrible freight or dread. Human beings desire security and almost everywhere throughout the world, their lot in life is insecurity. The connections with Rousseau's social contract seemingly, displayed that the problem of "freedom" and the problem of "security" for human beings in society are basically the same problem looked at from two opposite angles. Visible there are two distinct sources of personal insecurity in the present day society--(1) crime and (2) politics. It is also revealed from the performances of the state, the law and organised society in general that such authorities and agencies can provide only very limited protection against threats to personal security. Crime being a basic manifestation of human individuality and illegal politics rising to a challenge reveals the state's own ambiguity, the crime control machineries become successful only partly in their job.

Terrorism acquired a new dimension in the recent years throughout the world. Today terrorism has become part of daily events. The headlines of Daily newspapers on terrorist's attack horrified the minds of citizens and peace loving persons. Waves of terrorism may roll over the surface and tempest rage, but deep down there is the stratum of infinite calmness, infinite peace and infinite bliss. It is unheard of anyone achieved anything worth with blood lust, but anything can be achieved resorting to the path of Universal love. Terrorism has become a chronic problem due to its sustainance throughout the world.

Terrorism manifests itself in political, religious and socio-economic inequalities and exploitation. It thrives on grievances, real or imaginary when the state on the ruling oligarchy fails to redress injustices, infringement of rights of oppression. So long as the economic, social and racial indignities remain, the terror per se always be there. Terrorism has been used by political, religious, nationalistic and ethnic groups and by Government themselves. It is mainly a product of injustices prevailing in society. It is very grief to notice that terrorism affects and mars the growth and development everywhere. It has no territory, no religion, all forms of terrorism, its manifestations, committed wherever, whenever and by whomsoever as a profound threat to the peace, prosperity and security of all people of all faith of all nations as described by twenty one member of Sanghai Meeting held on 21st, October, 2001 after the dastardly terrorist attack on the world Trade Centre in New York killing over 7000 persons from Sixty different countries. The USA was specially interested in winning from this significant gathering dominated by Asian Nations, unrestricted support for military action in Afghanistan.

By 10 O' clock on the morning of September 11, Tuesday would become the worst terrorist attack in the history of the world. The first hijacked passenger jet American Airlines Flight 11 out of Boston, Massachusetts at 8.45 A.M., on September 11 crashed into the North Tower of the World

Trade Centre turning a gapping hole in the tower and setting it on fire the hijacked airliner, United Airlines Flight 175 from Boston just within 18 minutes at 9.30 A.M, crashes into the South Tower of the world Trade Centre and explodes. The same day at 9.30 A.M. American Airlines Flight 77 crashes into the Pentagon sending a huge plume of smoke. The Fourth United Airlines Flight 93 also hijacked, crashes in Somerset country, Pennsylvania. At 10-30 A.M. the South Tower of the World Trade Centre collupses plummeting into the streets below. Soon thereafter at 10.28 A.M. the north Tower of the World Trade Centre collupse from the top to down as it were being peeled apart. There were almost 43000 people employed in the twin tower complex having 110 storey covering a height of 1362 feet.

Osama Bin Laden, a Saudi engineer who is the leader of the Pentagon Attack volunteered to work for the CIA, used to tell the Americana who trained him in special operations that the so called had defeated on superpower and thereafter it would be the turn of the other superpower, The Pentagon was choosen as a target to show the world that the terrorist can strike at the heart of the US military command and control. The World Trade centre towers were presumably choosen since its destruction would hit three notionalists which the terrorists hate American, Israeli and Indians and cause large casualties among them. Though immediately after dastardly attack of Islamic terrorist on world Trade centre and Pentagon, George W. Bush, The president of America declared a massive plan to capture the leader of the terrorist group, Osama Bin Laden, has diverted its attention from Afghanistan Osama Bin Laden towards Iraq Sadam Hussain, the Islamic fundamentalists terrorists supported and abetted by Pakistan. The Islamic terrorists have also changed and choosen the soft centre for attack like Akshardham temple in Gandhinagar, Gujarat.

Attack on Jammu and Kashmir Assembly on Oct., 1, 2001 and on Parliament House, New Delhi, the symbols of power on 13 December, 2001 by Islamic terrorists were to demoralise a nation. The attack being not worked toward fulfilment of their aim, they changed the strategy to attack religious symbols, the sinister plan being the provoke sectarian violence. They mastermind for destabilising India which might be the reason for the attack on the Swaminarayan Temple to rock Gujarat again after horrified fallout of Godhra. The Inter service Intelligence (ISI) of Pakistan is know to have been behind the serious of bombing cases all over India during the last several years. The same agency also supported those who organised the serial bombing in Bombay in 1993 killing more then 500 persons. The hijacking of the Indian Airlines Flight 814 from Nepal was another case of terrorist, activities committed by the same group from across the border. The problem of terrorism and the problem of combating it is nothing new to India. India has been fighting against terrorism for more than a decade, but the enormity of the crime committed in New York has made the whole world share our concern. It is now widely admitted that punishing Osama Bin Laden and his Al-Qaeda organisation will not be enough. All the related terrorists organisations like -Jaish-e-Mohamed. Lakshar-e-Taiba, Hizbul-Mujahdeen. Babbar Khalsa International etc., at international level and all the terrorist organisations sustained within India at national level must be completely wiped out, if the problem of terrorism is to be settled once for all.

The world woke up to the reality of International terrorism since 11th September, 2001 when the condemnable terrorist attacks by the Al-Qaida Syndicate on the World Trade Centre and the pentagon strike at the heart of globalisation. There are several countries like Pakistan which still maintain double standard on terrorism. Pakistan fights the global war against terrorism on its western borders, but continues to harbour terrorism on its eastern borders in Jammu and Kashmir. The battle in Jammu and Kashmir today is between democracy and terrorism.

The North East States in India are also not less staggering in terrorism than in other parts of the country and outside Immediately after independence insurgency commenced in Nagaland and gradually spread to other areas. On 22 and March 1956 the Naga National Council (NNC) proclaimed the independent "Naga Federal Government" under the leadership of Phizo and insurgency commenced in an organised manner. With the signing of the Shillong Accord in November, 1975, Nagaland is a comparatively quiet state and in elections held in Nov. 1982 the INC(I) has been returned to power. But a group of Naga rebels is still in neighbouring Burma and has plans to start fresh incursion at an opportune time. On March 1. 1966 it was the turn of Mizo National Front lead by Laldenga to raise the banner of revolt against the Government and started a revolt almost on the Nagaland pattern. The trouble in Manipur was signalled by Meitei insurgency in June, 1978 under the leadership of Biseswar and the people's Liberation Army (PLA) and a little later by the People's Revolutionary Party of Kanglepak (PREPAK), a Marxist Leninist organisation under the leadership of Tulachandra. The Tripura Tribals revolted in June, 1980 against the lose of political power caused by an influx of Bengalis from Bangladesh which reduced them to a minority as well as subjecting them to Bengali economic domination which led to the alienation of their land, they are being deprived of jobs and exploited in trade. The Tripuri Upajati Juba Samity (TUJS) formed in 1967 has been agitating for restoration of tribal land, the deportation of foreigners and the creation of an autonomous district council for tribals, Tripura poses the most serious problem of ethnic harmony in the region.

Assam, the senior partner and a base of the Indian National Congress upto 1977 came under the grip of an agitation led by All Assam Students Union (AASU) and All Assam Ganga Sangram Parishad (AAGSP) over the Foreign national issue in 1979, an agitation which has caused serious damage to the national economy as well as national, unity. The democratic process which was virtually suspended was restored with election to the State Assembly in February, 1983. But it has generated divisive forces in the State on a scale that surpasses even these at the time of partition of Assam in 1947. The 1983 election in Assam saw the bloodiest election in India's electoral history. With the Separation of Nagaland, Maghalaya, Mizoram and Arunachal Pradesh, the State's area shrunk from 2,23,590 sq. km. to 78,523 sq.km. while the population increased in geometrical proportion, thereby disturbing the favourable land-man ratio and generating social tension. Moreover the mounting unemployment and inclusion of lakhs of foreigners in the voters list has become a red flag to a bull. By 1971 Assam found itself burdened with as many as 4,13,029 immigrants, posing a serious security risk and threatening the change the demographic profile of this frontier state. That the 4,13,029 immigrants would remain a permanent liability of Assam became apparent when the Union Government signed an agreement with the Bangladesh Government anyone having entered Assam prior to 25th March 1971 would not be accepted by Bangladesh.

The global, national and regional scenarios of terrorism from Al-Qaida to ULFA, BLT indicates that terrorism is a most serious problem of the hour and its effective control at the levels deems fit either through overpowering with legal provisions or by negotiation is the need of the day. At the same time the political indulgences on such terrorist activities with discrepancies and divergences with a view to fulfiling their selfish ends should be stopped at any cost with full participation of people at large. The prevailing provisions of terrorist Laws like TADA, POTA etc. are seems only partially effective. The permanent solution of the problem of terrorism needs a pre-emptive action.

21

Role of Governors in the Federal Wheel

The Governor of a State occupies in his State a position parallel to that of the President of the Union of India. In addition to ceremonial function, the Governor has been empowered to safeguard the Constitution and for this purpose he has been entrusted with a formidable armoury of powers. But, political trends and events developed regularly in each State have now lent heat to the debate and emerged on a critical need to re-examine the Governor's role in relation to both Constitutional theory and practical politics. The position of the Governor after Independence has drastically changed". The literal reading of the provision of our Constitution indicates that the Governor emerges as the least secure and the least protected of all Constitutional functionaries like the President of India, a Judge of the Supreme Court or a Judge of a High Court etc. The President of India can be removed from his office only by impeachment for violation of the Constitution after following the elaborate procedure provided in Article 61 of the Constitution. Similarly the Judge of the Supreme Court or a High Court can be removed from his office only on the ground of proved misbehaviour or incapacity and after an address by each House of Parliament, supported by majority of total membership of the House and by a majority of not less than two thirds of the members of that House present and voting has been presented in the same session for the removal as per provision of Article 124(4), 217. Same procedure is also to be followed in case of removal of the Comptroller and Auditor General of India and the Election Commissioner (Art. 48 and 224). Art. 317 of the Constitution provides provision for removal of the Chairman or a member of the Union Public Service Commission on the ground of misbehaviour after the Supreme Court on a reference being made in it by the President, has on enquiry arrived at a finding of misbehaviour. Such type of security of tenure is not available to the Governor, the Head of a State.

Art. 155 of the Constitution says that the Governor of a State shell be appointed by the President by warrant under his hand and seal' and Art. 156(1) of the Constitution provides provision that the Governor shall hold Office during the pleasure of the President. Provisions of both these Articles creates some controversies. Literal interpretation of the provisions of Article 155 and 156(1) indicates that the Governor; of a State is an appointee of the Central Government, as the appointing authority, that is the President of India acts on the advice of his Council of Ministers and therefore subordinate to the Central Government. There is a widespread belief that the Governor functions covertly or though it may be as an agent of the Central Government and acts with the prior approval of the Central Ministries. Governor's role played from time to time in many cases in different States created reasons to believe on such contention. A fierce controversy arised on the role played by the former Governor of Andhra Pradesh, Ram Lal and before him the Governor of Jammu and Kashmir, Jagmohan through the action they took in the content of the Chief Minister loosing in majority in the legislature. There are some differences in detail between the two cases, but the essentials are the same. Both these cases cannot absolve one from the responsibility of analysing the situations from the legal and Constitutional point of view, in order to obviate similar situations in future or if necessary change the provisions of the Constitution. This is what the rule -of law demands.

While Art. 74 of the Constitution enjoins that the President 'shall in exercise of his functions act in accordance with the advice' given by the Council of Ministers heeded by the Prime Minister, no such corresponding obligation is cast on the Governor of a State, in relation to the advice of the State Cabinet headed by the Chief Minister (Art. 163). Thus the Governor's lattitude of discretion is clearly more than that of the President. The Governor and his role in the federal wheel under the Indian Constitution is guided by Art. 157-164. These Articles of the Constitution provide as follows:

1. There shall be a Governor for each State.
2. The Executive powers of the State shall vest in the Governor.
3. The Governor shall be appointed by the President and shell hold Office during the latter's pleasure.
4. The Governor shall appoint the Chief Minister of the State.
5. The Chief Minister holds Office at the pleasure of the Governor, and
6. The Council of Ministers shall be collectively responsible to the State legislative Assembly.

Since the Governor appoints the Chief Minister and the Council of Ministers is collectively responsible to the legislative Assembly, a convention has been developed in the country, harmonising these two provisions. In practice after every election, the Governor appoints the leader of the political party returned in a majority to the Assembly as the Chief Minister. In the system of appointment of the Chief Minister of the State the Governor as the Executive heed has to face multiferous problems under a varied circumstances as appeared in many States, particularly in those where majority prevails by a party other than the Ruling party at the Centre and in case of defection. It will be prudent for the Governor to take all the relevant aspects into consideration while taking decisions which he is called upon to take under the provisions of the Constitution. Generation of controversy which is not desirable should always be avoided. In the process of executive functionaries of the States in India, the question of Centre-State relations acquired great importance in the context of the growing alienation between the Centre and the constituent States. To stop the process of alienation between the Centre and the constituent units of the Indian Union is therefore urgently necessary in the interest of Indian Unity.

During the period from 1950 to 1967, the Governors were functioning as a mere Constitutional heads of States without facing any serious problem of applying discretionary powers. But, after 1967, several Governors exercised their discretionary powers extensively, to cite examples, in West Bengal in 1967; in Punjab in 1969 and in 1970; and in Haryana in 1982. In the recent past, the conduct of some Governors, particularly in Sikkim, Pondichery, Jammu and Kashmir and Andhra Pradesh has been so deplorable that it has shaken the confidence of people, not only in the functioning of the Constitution of India, but also in the democratic process itself. Under all the circumstances the application of the doctrine of pleasure and discretionary power is to be made very cautiously within the Constitutional boundaries.

22

India's Nuclear Blue Print and the Global Order

On August 6, when the end of the World War II was already in sight, the United States dropped an atomic bomb on the Japanese city of Hiroshima. A second bomb was dropped on an another Japanese city Nagasaki three days later. The explosive power of each of those bombs was estimated at 15.25 thousand tons of TNT. The blast wave, high concentration of heat and resultant fires destroyed houses and structures over an area of 8.12 square kilometers. About two lakh people died in the blasts in two Japanese cities. This was the first threat of nuclear weapons prevailed in the international order. The subsequent development of nuclear weapons proceeded in several directions improving gradually from kiloton range to megaton range. Stockpiling of these thermonuclear bombs definitely hove reason to cause concern for all nations.

India has been campaigning for last ten years for an effective nuclear disarmament. But its appeal on that score having fallen on deaf ears and the security environment around it having progressively worsened due to several factors including growing potentiality of nuclear blackmail as a result of collaborative action between Beijing and Islamabad enjoying Washington's indulgence. India was left with practically no alternative, but to exercise the nuclear option in its fundamental national interest. India's spirited response to the UN Security Council resolution denouncing the nuclear test is praiseworthy and appropriate. Under no circumstance a double standard nuclear policy of the world acceptable to all notions. Specially when the charges against the two largest South Asian States who are far more guilty of the same occasion have been levelled by the very nations in the present conflict have not been responded, the coercive moves by P-5 cannot browbeat. India's standing and capability into meek submission. If the task of nuclear disarmament is to be carried out in right earnest the South Asian neighbours have to dedicate themselves for the purpose of preserving and promoting universal peace and the neighbouring countries of India have to resorted a creative cooperation instead of destructive confrontation.

Disarmament and prevention of a thermonuclear war are among the most acute and urgent problems of today. They ore a matter of vital concern for, all nations. The measures for disarmament if taken effectively on an international scale without bias attitude towards the imperialist countries help to reduce the danger of a new world war. But this danger remains great. The reactionary circles in the imperialist countries are continuing their stockpiling of weapons of mass destruction. Let us now turn to the issue of sanctions imposed on India by America. Are such sanctions really permissible under the various global legal orders. From the issues from the past we seem assume that the nuclear nations have a unilateral right to impose collective sanctions, where does this right come from? In respect of the sanctions neither the substantive law nor its procedural requirements have been complied with. The Pokhran explosions under no circumstance a greater threat to global peace than are the already armed and ready nuclear death squad nations of America, England, France, Russia and Chine. If we go through the relevant laws we find that the notions required by the law and policy does not fulfil threated sanctions and to take over global financial institutions to force a moratorium on aid, support and leans. It is not India's a nuclear testing that was illegal, it is the sanctions that ore being sought to be imposed are illegal and this type of exercise may be interpreted re international bullying with little justification and legality. Development of nuclear technology does not produce any threat to global peace. Nuclear power is required to develop a nation in all directions. Nuclear energy can be used both for development and destruction purposes whatever be the aim of its use for preparation of weapons or peaceful exploitation, the proof of and use results is a dire need. Nuclear testing is a process of proving the and use results. One of the important peaceful application of atomic energy is the, use of radioisetopes in industry, agriculture, medicine, feed preservation, hydrology, oceanography and a host of other disciplines. Radioisetopes have already started playing a very significant role in Indian industry. One of the important applications has been in the determination of the movement of silt on sea bed at various harbours using the radioisotope tracer technique. As a result of such studies the port authorities concerned have saved considerable amounts of money in dredging operations. Besides, the tracer technique has been also used for the detection of leaks in buried pipes, co-exial cables and dams, for measuring of river flows and for investigating underground water resources. Another important area in which radioisotopes are increasingly being applied is in determining the quality of Industrial products using what is known as radiography method. In the field, of agriculture, besides basic research on the effect of radiation on plants and their products, plant mutation breeding programme can be undertaken by use of radioisotopes. Several mutants of scientific and economic importance have already been isolated. These include strains of rice with much favourable characteristics as high yield, fine grain, early flowering etc. Ionising radiation like gamma rays provide an effective means for food preservation since they can inhibit the growth and metabolism of food borne spoilage organisms as well as eradicate insect posts in stared grains. In the field of medicine, application of radioisotopes and the radiation they emit in the diagnosis and treatment of diseases is an important use of nuclear energy. These are some of the peaceful uses of nuclear energy developed within the country through dedicated research by Indian scientists and technologists.

The Pokhran tests certainly a clear demonstration of the sophistication of India's technological competence. The capability of nuclear power generation of the country is needed both for self defence from external aggression as well as for the country's self development and self economic reliance with peaceful uses of such power. The attempts of the nuclear death squad nations to keep the Indian nuclear capabilities under wraps forever is not prudential and cannot be justified. The presumption that the nuclear blasts in the sub-continent last month hove fundamentally challenged the structure of the global nuclear order has conflicted with the Practice and pretence of the order and its presumption that the world will be governed forever by a "five and no more nuclear weapon". Unbiasly the global order could acknowledge India and Pakistan's reality and accommodate them as declared nuclear weapon powers in the global atomic order.

23

Space Technology: Their Legal Implication and Future Development

Space technology nowadays getting much importance nationally as well as internationally as new achievements and discoveries in this field can be used for the benefit and peaceful purposes of mankind. The ever increasing complicated problems of mankind arising out of copulation growth is possible only through use of advance science and technology like spacecraft, Nuclear science etc. So, an effective planning for development of this important field is needed for economic re-generation and future existence of mankind.

The question may arise why India has made and sent up satellite instead of growing more food or digging more wells. But it is surprising to know that satellite and food ere very much inter-related. For growing more food, we need more accurate data on soil and water resources. The data can be gathered by satellites in a scientific manner, yielding several advantages. It is particularly useful where information is required repeatedly over a vast under more or less uniform lighting conditions. Cameras on satellite can see much more then the naked eye. They can for instance spot a diseased crop, much before the farmer on the ground could notice it.

So far as the question of air space is concerned, the

responsibility to make all-out efforts to see that new avenues and fresh resources are properly and adequately utilised, lies on the U.N. The important legal implication of space activities is that, the States can utilise air space in way of its exploration for the benefit and useful purposes of mankind—for furthering the causes of human happyness, progress and prosperity and at the same time avoidance of fresh factors of conflict, rivalry and exploitation of the weaker by the stronger. The State exploring the outer space exercise complete control over it. The other States can get some rights over it only through some governments or treaties. There is no customary rule of International Law in regard to giving innocent passage through the territorial air space. Man has not yet been able to ascertain through the satellite launching as to what metallic or any other kind of valuable articles or properties, if any will be available in outer space, the moon and other celedtial bodies. The peaceful uses of Cuter Space treaty of 1966 has rightly emphasised on avoidance of harmful contamination and adverse changes in, the environment of the Earth in the exploration and use of the outer space and the celestial bodies.

Now we are to consider the need of expanding scientific research in the totality of space. The scope for such research in literally limitless. We are not even sure what constitutes the ultimate frontiers of space or indeed whether there are any and so in absolute terms we are in moving away from the Earth with man-made instrumentation. With a satellite built for use in Earth orbit or a probe designed to penetrate for deeper into space, there are certain aspects of the spacecraft which has no problem for operation in any particular part of space. An effective generation development and use of space technology for future prospects depends on the environment in which satellite equipment is required to operate. When the choice of probes is made that go towards the Sun, naturally thermal environment is on increasing problem. So, the choice has to be made between probes needing a long life so that repetitive scientific measurements can be taken and probes that can be cent towards the Sun bent on self destruction—probes with no long-term future which will ultimately melt and plunge into the solar gravitational field which will have captured them. Both, the probes go towards the Sun and going away from the Sun have certain disadvantages. The former require equipments that can withstand high temperature as the Sun *is* approached. But the importance of the mission must justify the cost. In both of these cases, however a greet challenge arises for the technologists making such spacecraft to provide materials that can withstand the temperatures and provide environmental control system that will carry heat away from sensitive areas and radiate the excess into space. To this extent the presence of a spacecraft in the vacuum environment or near vacuum environment of space is an advantage, as the temperatures received by a probe are those arising from the direct radiant heat from the Sun felling on all ports of the craft facing it.

Considering the effectiveness of technologies so far developed in ell the aspects of space travel performance, the future plan of research on space activities may be decided with the experience gathered at home and abroad. Now it open to many new ideas which are certainly in evidence with regard to the expansion of research programmes away from the Earth and greater knowledge of the planets of our solar system and beyond. There is a limitless amount of scientific data to be pursued and indeed some of the results of the probes of the next few years will gibe better pointers as to where the main thrust of research in the future should best take place.

Space technology will be the most appropriate technology having no alternative to coop up the problems of our survival. The direct application of space technology for communication, navigation and resources survey are of immense importance to the world community measured in economic, sociological, political, industrial, commercial and other terms. The application of men-made satellite in communication had been foreseen as far beck as 1945. The value of the use of satellite for navigation and Earth observation purposes has already developed since the beginning of the space are in 1857. Along with other advanced countries, India has been able to develop satellite communication system and already has been a world leader in conjunction with the United Nations and the U.S.A. in the SITE experiment. In future, India's considerable land masses coupled with its vast population could make excellent use of the facilities available from communication system. The scope for use of satellite technology in navigation is limited in comparison to communication. The financial implications are also interesting in the range of possibilities that can be anticipated. We have already primary and secondary application areas to watch in the use of satellites for navigational purposes.

The use of satellite communication system in observation of Earth's resources have already reached massive dimensions in both commercial and strategic respects. The amount and value of data can be obtained from images obtained from spacecraft are orders greater than the data that have for years been gathered from aircraft carrying cameras etc. By using spacecraft, massive amount of informations relevant to many features covering c wide spectrum of activity con be gathered within a short time which is not possible from aircraft, the next effective communication vehicle. We have every reason to be pleased therefore that the space ere has been launched with such diverse and successful applications of space using automatic spacecraft of growing ingenuity, complexity and reliability. At the same time the International treaties, Agreements and conventions acceptable to the majority must be worked out in the procedures of entry to outer space and the cosmos, exploration and use for peaceful purposes making binding on all. There should be some sort of penal provisions in case of every Treaty or Agreement. The problem of inadequate sanction on machinery for application or enforcement of panel provision in International Law should be solved through International Agreements and understandings.

24

Land Use Change and Global Environment

Land is scarce resource of the world. The changing of population, economic, social pattern and scientific development lead to a drastic change in land use throughout the world. In the last few centuries and particularly in the last several decades efforts of land use change have become global. Change in land use reflect not only the history, but also the future of mankind. They are linked with economic development, population growth, technology and the total environmental change. Tremendous work on land use change and its impact on the environment have so far done in different parts of the world. The change takes place due to various factors such as multiplication of population of human being and animals, geomorphological changes and development climactic variations and fluctuation of other natural activities.

Human activities are a major factor contributing to global change and they are ever riding natural changes to ecosystems brought on by climate variations of the past few thousand years. At the annual meeting of the Ecological Society of America held in August, 1992 a symposium highlighted key research issues in land use and land cover change. Human activities have resulted many changes in the environment. Some of the important activities responsible for changes in environment are land management practice for Agriculture and forestry, rerouting of hydro logical flows introduction of exotic species industrial contamination of land, water and air, constructions of building, roads etc. space use and unclear production activities industrial emissions during the last century throughout the world have rapid altered atmospheric competition as evidenced by the increasing acid deposition rates in Europe and North America and by the increasing atmospheric concentration of ozone depleting gases such as carbon dioxide and chlorof crocarbon.

Land management practices such as fine grazing and tilling effect ecosystem composition, cycling of nutrients and distribution of organic matter. In research paper of "Human transformation of the earth's vegetation cover pest and future impacts of agricultural development and climatic change" presented by W.C. Clark, J Richards and E. Flint in a workshop held at NASA, green belt during 27-29th January, 1986 it was indicated that, over the pest 120 years, land conversion to cropland has significantly altered major blames globally.

Growing human population causes increased pressure on terrestrial ecosystem as demands increase for each resources as food, fuel, fiber and water. Such human demands are increasing day by day and affects the global environment. Pressure of population in one region of the world affects in other regions by deteriorating the climatic conditions on terrestrial ecosystems.

Regional differences in technological capacity and wealth will affect the impact of climate and land use change in coming decades. Social and economic forces within a region often dictate how land is used. The imbalance of future conditions prevailed due to land use practices developed over a long period under different environmental, political, demographic and social conditions. The factors controlling land use change vary according to social political, economic characteristics. The response to human activities to environmental changes will be contingent on the productivity of the land. In some cases, the environmental changes may enhance productivity and others, the change may be degrade resources. The study of social environment promoting land management help in educating people to promote social behaviour and social status. In developing countries, high population growth causes increases demand on commercialization and mobilisation of resources for economic development.

Such demands contribute to increase use of lands for agricultural purpose with inappropriate climates. This expansion is placing unprecedented pressures on their natural environments.

Local and regional land use and land cover change is an important ingredient in changing the global climate and biosphere. Land cover change effect biodiversity, trees gas emissions and other factors that cumulatively alter the global climate. A thorough study on the pattern of land use and land cover change is needed to analyse the social and political forces that can be linked to other types of environmental simulations. Such type of research can provide the ways and means of balancing the ecological environment with the acquired capability to predict.

Plant diversity is a common phenomena in natural ecosystems and in farmer field. From time immemorial, people have identified economic plant species and conserved them in different parts of the world. With a view to raising economic prosperity, planting and cultivation of economic plants under variable conditions of soil and land in different countries is an ongoing activity. In developing countries most of the diversity of the cultivated plant species is maintained by poor marginal subsistence farmers under mixed multiple cropping systems, for their livelihood and for personal use. The pattern of land use and land cover change depends upon the prevailing system of cultivation and subsisted conditions.

Alongwith other parts of the world, rapid changes in land use and land cover took place in India during last century and more prominently during last two deades. During last two decades a new approach for determining land use changes has appeal. With the help of satellite communication, direct measurement of areas of different types of land cover and the changes in this cover has become possible. In our country, the organisation like National Remote Sensing Agency, nowadays helps in measuring land use change, various aspects like forestry, hydrology, geomorphology etc.

25

Population and Hunger: Possibilities and Expectations

The worldwide interest in development reflects a deep concern about the existence of so much of poverty in an age when the application of science and technology could substantially lessen if not abolish it. Approximately three-fourths of the world's people live below the poverty line. The real poverty is predominant in low income countries. The situation is now further worsen due to prevailing economic crisis and population explosion in all the countries. Associated with population increase, are needlessly low life expectancy, food crisis, nutritional deficiency and high infant mortality. Furthermore income is heavily concentrated in a wealthy few in most of the countries like India. Concentration of money in the hands of a wealthy few is a mechanism existed in the process of exploitation. If production is equal to demand, there are good chances that nobody will be in a position to exploit the situation. If production is less than demand, consumers are able to exploit producers. After all we need a stable economy in the country to cope up the problems of food, hunger and employment. The best way to achieve this is by enhancing production where it falls short of demand and reducing it or exporting it where it is above domestic demand. With these objects a network of laws to control economy in India at the point of production, supply as well as distribution on the spot have been developed, but of little avail. It has to be understood that not the wage or salary income but the profit income is the chief source of economic injustice in the country.

A large number of people in India are producing Agricultural products, e.g. wheat, rice, gram, pluses, vegetables, fruits, spices, sugarcane, cotton, oilseeds etc. Farmers have often been complaining that they are allowed lesser rate of profit as compared to their industrial counterparts. Since this opinion was held by a large section, it attracted legislative attention. The increase in prices of their produce would have hit the poor. So, attempts were made in the beginning to control the prices of agricultural inputs. Hence Fertilizer Control Order was issued in 1957. The order provided for fixation of maximum prices of which a manufacturer or dealer may sell different categories of fertilizer by the central government. It also provided for registration of dealers and fertilizer mixtures. Later by adopting the practice of fixing a supporting price for agricultural products, the need of delegated legislation for controlling price of these commodities has been dispensed with. Thus the prices fixed for wheat, rice, gram, coarse grain, jute, sugarcane etc. are not part of law, but the result of an administrative action. Justice Krishna Iyer once pointed out that "Today a black marketeer can become an officially honoured philanthropist, which is demoralising". The main objective of passing Food Corporation Act, 1964 to establish a machinery to procure sufficient amount of foodgrains etc. to be used as a reserve to bring down the prices if the grain merchants choose to exploit the situation have been practically defeated, price hike continued to be prevailed.

During the twenty first century, it should be possible

to raise the level of living gradually above the minimum existence level, if population growth is slowed down substantially in one hand and improvement in science and technology are largely used for production of foodgrains and essential commodities instead of production of luxuries for a few and military hardwares on the other hand. The rate of scientific and technological progress today is largely determined by the speed with which the instruments and means of labour are changing. The growing impact of science on production brought a fundamental change in the technology of production. The important role played by agricultural sciences and the introduction of new technological means and methods of production control necessitate new systems of training and qualifying workers .instructors in the field of agricultural in order to keep up production with increase in the number of population. Scientific and technological progress will help liquidate narrow specialisation. However, a rapid ride in the technological level of working people in the field of agriculture is impossible today without specialisation, because the mastery of a new speciality in the present conditions provides for the acquisition of a certain amount of knowledge, skill and professional know-how.

The food we eat gives us the energy that we need to do our jobs. It builds up the body, in fact it keeps us alive. If we do not get sufficient intake of calories through food to satisfy our hunger and fulfil our energy outputs, we ere said to be underfed, we also needs protein and vitamins to build up the body. Children, especially require them to build strong bones and muscles as they are growing. If we do not get enough of these proteins, vitamins and minerals, we are said to be undernourished. The developed countries of the world have and will continue to have "the capacity to manage their affairs smoothly and in case of food shortage of these countries, can import from others where available. But, the poor countries do not have enough money to pay for food imports, they are dependent on aid from richer nations and if they do not get it, they will die, Britain has never suffered from widespread and long lasting famine although there have been chronic food shortages. One of the reasons for this is that throughout the long history, most of the wars that it has fought have taken place beyond its shores. In Ireland, potato blight caused the potato crop of 1845 and 1846 to fail miserably. This led to widespread famine and the death of nearly one million people. But the increase in scientific farming methods that began with the Agricultural revolution has ensured that the days of hunger have long since gone from most of Europe. The famine in sub-Sahara region of Africa which is popularly known as Sahel and encompassed many African nations frcm Mauritania and Senegal to Mali, Volta, Niger, Chad and Ethiopia was the worst of present century. The disaster occurred during 1973 and 1974 when one million died of hunger, malnutrition and diseases aggravated by hunger and malnutrition. In India, the Bengal famine of 1943 is bound to go down in the history of this sub-continent as the most gruesome tragedy of the present century. In this disaster nearly three million people were allowed to die within the span of one year. India was at that time under British rule. A colonial power subsists only on exploitation of the resources of the ruled nation. They have naturally, no interest in the welfare of the ruled people. Canada and Australia were reedy to send wheat, but the British Government did not accept the offer on the plea of shortage of ships to transport it to India, when Relief and Rehabilitation Committee of the United Nations started distributing foodgrains to war ravaged countries. Bengal was excluded from its purview on the plea that Bengal does not qualify as war ravaged area.

Alongwith the problem of food shortages to feed the prospective population, malnutrition and its associated diseases prevails in countries like Africa, India and other third world countries. Better food is the instrument, but better nutrition is also the objective, in India, the spread of, malnutrition coincides with population explosion and moved from countryside to cities. Many drifted to the towns and cities, these loft behind continued to try to support themselves from their small holdings. Solution of food problem needs both short term and long term programme. The long term solution is probably two fold—population control and development of new crops with productive utilisation of barren lands and waște lands. The short term solution include modernisation of cultivation, multiple cropping, mixed farming etc. Although many of the broad objectives of Agricultural policies appear to have been achieved, it is not clear how much is due to the policies themselves and how much to other factors. India has in the four decades since Independence, a formal and comprehensive resolution on the agricultural policy. The pre-ocupation has been with ensuring food supplies and that generally through measures of short-term expediency. Lastly, a National Policy on Agriculture came out in 1990 as per advice of The Standing Advisory Committee on Agriculture (SAC) constituted by the Government of India in March, 1989. Now we expect that, implementation of National Agricultural Policy will enhance production to commensurate with population increase.

26

Deforestation and Environmental Degradation

One of the most profligate use of woodland in recent times has been the conversation of wood land into house land. In the developing countries wood is an important fuel and will be for many decades to come. For many poor people it takes a whole day to collect fuel for the next day's cooking. At present India is severely effected by the problem of forest devastation and the resulting unbalances in the ecological system. In many forest areas tribal are allowed to take from the forest whatever they can carry, trees are felled, allowed to rot and then carried away as dead wood which is not recorded in forest department statistics. Timber contractors and smugglers take their own toll of the woods. As a result, once densely wooded areas of Rajasthan, Assam and some other absorb water and bind the soil particles. In the areas of deforestation such binding forces of soil particles last. So the denuded areas have been experiencing flash floods. Deforestation endangered the dry regions where biomass production is limited by the tropical highlands.

Effect of trees on local climate is an another important aspect in changing the environment. The high density of trees in a forest area reduces the maximum air and soil temptress while retaining a high relative humidity even during dry season. Thus the conditions of a dense forest are like that of a green house warm and humid. For this reason maintaining a higher density of tree cover in a park is needed to cater to human comfort. The beneficial effect of forest in decreasing the amount of evaporation from soil is well known. Bare soils and land covered without plants practically cease to evaporate after a few rainless days, while green leafed forests continue to transpire for many more days, depending on the amount of soil water reserves. Trees accept large amounts of rain in their canopy and this is rapidly evaporated back to the atmosphere. Another notable effect of forest on climate is that, a thick cover of trees reduce the speed of wind and help people in sheltering during cyclones. The intensive damage caused by cyclones in recent years is due to the denudation of forests. When the soil is not protected by a Tree cover, torrential rains cause heavy erosion losses. Also higher soil temperatures increase the rate of mineralisation of the organic matter present increase in it. This increased mineralisation action impairs the stability of soil structure and make it easily erodable.

Fuel wood is one of the important source of energy. Fuel wood is not limited to household use. It has tremendous use in fuel machines. The lumber and paper industries have long used bark and waste to generate steam and electricity. Growing trees for firewood can be successfully combined with the production of posts, police and timber. It has been estimated that at least 75 per cent of tropical land is inherently unsuited to sustained conventional agriculture, but 35 per cent of the population of the tropic lives on this land. About half of them will not support vegetation of any kind. The best use of the reminder is tree cultivation with annual crops or with the pasturing of animals. In India the rural poor, particularly in remote villages where LPG, Kerosene and coal are hard to come by are mostly dependent on fuel wood. Such fuel wood they receive from forests. Nowadays indiscriminate felling of trees in forest has led to fresh floods, soil erosion and silting of dams. As a result floods are unchecked, electricity generation hampered and irrigation supply disturbed. It this phenomenon of forest devastation continue to unchecked by strong action by the government, the demand for fuel wood, building and other programmes will be outstripped. The quickest solutions are fuel wood plantation to meet the demand and effective legislation to protect forest resources. The National Forest Policy of India advocates that 33 per cent of total land areas should be under forest to meet the growing demand of fuel, energy and other uses of wood. But, at present only 22 per cent is reported to be under forest. There is thus an additional 10 per cent of land could be brought under forests.

Any plantation programme whether in public sector or in private sector, people's participation is invariably required. The control on forest devastation by the government can provide plans, money and advice. But unless people are made to realise the importance of raising plantations specially in community lands such a programme will not be fruitful. So have now reached the stage of planning the fuel wood other biomass production with a viable forest policy. This needs a comprehensive quantitative input output analysis of the factors which determine biomass yields. The present level of analysis as well as the production programme is inadequate in comparison to the rate of deforestation prevailed.

27

The Question of Individual Security in the Criminal Environment

Every individual in the present day society feels insecured due to the threat of the criminal environment developed in recent years. The crime in the present day society have been increasing day by day in a rampant way. She threat of insecurity of individuals prevail due to enhanced dimension of crimes in the one hand and individual's exposure to hostility and malevolent indifference of crime control machineries on the other. Insecurity of individuals results from inimical, damaging, irregular and unpredictable conduct in society, from lawlessness and disorder in general. Crime in society always vied with economic and social matters as the gravest public concern. Unemployment and economic problems may raise anxieties about, standard of living and well being, but crimes threatens life itself and potentially exposes everyone's person and property to risk from predators. The prevailing reaction of public to criminality is alarming and may be regarded as a form of moral panic. The daily newspapers, weeklies, fortnightlies and monthlies have the coverage with bold heads of news on incidence of crimes in various forms like murder, rape, abdication, kidnapping, thefts, dacoities and so on creating panic to public mind. The crime rates are increasing in such a way that disturbs the social and moral order and effects more person adversely. The trend of criminality now going on should not be allowed to continue in our society if we want the existence of our society.

As a matter of fact criminals are the victims of circumstances. We cannot afford to ignore the significance of the force of circumstances which moulds the pattern of behaviour of a criminal. Many persons specially the youngsters commit petty offences not because of any inherent criminal tendencies or not because of any guilty intention, but because of the fragrant situation that surrounds them and the lack of legitimate opportunities for achieving various ends in their lives. A guilty person must never go unpunished, but in awarding the punishment his environments, the circumstances of the case and the nature of the offence must be taken into consideration. I am of the view that even a cruel and hardened criminal can be converted into a helpful friend if he is treated lovely and sympathetically and got rid of the circumstances which were responsible for compelling him to commit the offence. In this respect the prime responsibility to bring out a drastic change in the minds of the criminals for averting a criminal holocaust lies with the State. Punishment has in some form or other been considered absolutely necessary to the maintenance of law and order. All eminent political philosophers have found for it some sort of moral justification. In the process of crime control through institutionalisation of punishment, an effective policing is necessary. The police are morally permitted and obligated to do things like coerce, forcibly arrest, incapacitate, injure, shoot, interrogate etc.; which would be forbidden in ordinary circumstances and might in fact responsible per se, yet at the same time its context elevates police work to become the highest embodiment and epitome of morality as such the first line defence of society at points where it is most vulnerable, its security against itself, punishment of criminal is pay law whatever its form and whatever label it might bear--execution person, banishment, flogging, fine, psychiatric treatment or community service signifies the putting of the will of the State that is the society in the abstract, against the individual, it is an imposition, however circumscribed, it is the infliction of pain, however mild or remote or as the threat of pain, hypothetical, without such punishment it is said the State would cease to function. The trouble is that a deal is not a deal if it cannot be enforced. Moreover when we really got down to it, fear force and pain are the only things that work.

Quite a great deal again has been written on the rationale and justification of punishment by the state and the respective merits and insights as well as inadequacies of the three most important theories—retribution, deterrence and reformation are well known. The first theory apparently permits the punishment of the innocent and punishment out of proportion to the gravity of the offence. Retribution seems to presuppose an assessment of world wickedness that is boy end the competence of the law to make and hence degeneration into macro revenge. It seems only to harden the criminals as an enemy of society. Deterrence and reformation are merely consequential notions and are logically expendable. Their presence might make the state's punitive actions more palatable, but they cannot supply the primary moral right to punishment. The assumption which legitimates state power as distinguished from the moral authority of the state is that there is a certain amount of hostility, conflict and malevolent indifference at large in society, but this amount is not overwhelming.

In dealing with crime, we may note that with the gaining ground of theory of determinism and development, radical school of penal reform, pathological and psychiatric remedies are ranking in the forefront. Out of two types of measures--re-educative and punishment against criminals, the former is beneficial in case of general criminals and the latter is appropriate in case of recidivists. An effective deal with the criminals is possible through liquidation of factors creating criminal behaviour of people particularly of young stars. Want of employment and growing and overgrowing population should be checked with perspective planning in short term and long term basis. In this direction a sincere effort of the government is a dire need. Those who are in-political field and power should give much interest on development of the State in all directions rather than self benefits.

It is time to embark on a bit of more serious effort on security of life and property. Security can well claim to be the chief human value, certainly for people as we know them and in the kind of society in which we live. Introspection experience in communication and reflective analysis would all tend to con-firm this. As the oxford English Dictionary defence it security means the condition of being protected from and being not exposed to danger, freedom from doubt or a state of self assurance, certainly well founded confidence and it means freedom from care anxiety and apprehension. The state ought to provide personal protection, ought to endeavour to maintain our personal safety. But it is not realistic to expect total protection, as the criminality arise, unpredictably in all kinds of societies. The state fulfils its duty if it contains crime by whatever means, keeps it at a low level and provides it were statistical protection. At the same time cisterns fulfils his or her duty by remaining law-abiding and by showing a certain amount of public responsibility by helping victims, reporting on crime, providing information, rejecting shelters to criminals etc.

There is a air of gloom, despair, sadness and

pointlessness surrounding beliefs, life style and conduct of political extremists groups and this again is a feature of negatively shared with the world of crime. This is like crime a permanent and unpredictable source of discomfort and definitely a threat to personal security. Their malevolent indifference to the actual wishes and desires of people outside, as a result their concern for justice and humanity is in effect indicting disable from the conduct of ordinary outlaws. Fanaticism and extremism may arise anywhere at any time in any circumstance. The law abiding citizen is no more responsible for their appearance than for the ubiquitous presence of criminality. Thus the control and suppression of crime and the provision of personal security against the threat posed by them lies inescapably with the state.

Considering all the aspects of criminality and its control the present and prospective governments in the centre as well as in States should prepare perspective plans to eradicate crimes from the society ensuring security of lives and property. Public participation in the respect is also an inevitable need.

Index

T

U

V

W

❑❑❑